The Promotable Woman

Have we come
a long way, baby?

By Jan Northup, Ph.D.

Portions of this book are based on the original video training program The Promotable Woman: What Makes The Difference created by Dr. Jan Northup and written by Dr. Jan Northup and Dana Evans Balibrera. Some activities are based on The Promotable Woman Resource Manual written by Sandi Strohmeier and edited by Dr. Jan Northup and Dana Evans Balibrera.

USA $19.99

Canada $24.99

ISBN 978-0-9796028-0-1

This book is
dedicated in memory
of two women
who had an
incredible impact on my life.
Ida Hurley,
my grandmother,
and
Dorothy Kratochwill,
a truly remarkable woman.

Acknowledgements

Okay, this is the page that will be read by my family, friends and colleagues to see if they got their names in print. If you are not a friend, family member or colleague, you can skip this page and go right to Chapter 1.

If you are someone who has really ticked me off, my attorney advised me that book sales might not cover any related legal fees so you don't even have to buy the book for your evidence, marked Exhibit A!

In all seriousness, I could not have completed this book without the past and present support of significant people in my life and acknowledge them at this time:

My mother who continues to be a role model of generosity and unconditional love and for giving me two wonderful and special sisters, Jayne Schweitzer and Dottie Woodard.

My son, Josh, who has been a joy and a teacher as I explored my values as a working mother.

Sheryl Stephen who has hung in there with me on yet another project as my right hand, left hand, my right brain and left brain (you get the idea) making sure my company kept on track so I could give my attention to writing.

Sandi Strohmeier who was my sounding board when I first had the idea of writing a book for women 22 years ago.

As in all of my serious, and some not so serious projects, she continues to be my creative partner by playing devil's advocate, contributing great ideas and activities and making a mean martini when a writer's block needs a break!

Dorothy O'Brien and Eydie Hiebert for taking time from their busy schedules to serve as readers on the book.

Don Easterly, alone we did so little and together we've done so much.

The thousands of women around the world who have inspired me, who have modeled the success factors of a promotable woman, and who have shared their personal "stories" with me, especially Lindsay Alcott, Dr. Lynda McNulty Lakin, Sandi Strohmeier, Eydie Hiebert, Kathy Wentworth Drahosz and McKenna Stephens.

Vickie Mullins of Mullins Creative, Inc. for another great job in preparing my work for print.

And last, but not least, a gentle and loving message for Tarzan, "Here's the deal. Hurry, call Dominos!"

Content

Introduction vii

1 | Prosperity Thinking 1

2 | Patterns for Power 23

3 | Positioning 45

4 | Prescriptions for Comfort Management 75

5 | Programming for Play 100

6 | Principal and Interest 119

7 | Purposing 147

About the Author 179

Introduction

Just The Facts

A book for women about professional success – Why today? This is a question that I asked 20 years ago and am asking again today. This isn't exactly the dawn of the women's movement nor is this the first book written specifically for women. The market has been flooded with self-help books for women. The subject of these books: How to achieve personal and professional success. Why are we still buying them? You would think now, in 2007, we'd have the magic answer, the quick fix or the "follow these easy steps and …". Women are still looking for ways to excel professionally while maintaining the traditional role of wife, partner, mother, daughter, sister, friend, community member and caregiver. They are still trying to gain equality as a professional in the workplace and in the paycheck.

The more I thought about the title of the book, I had to ask myself whether I truly believed that women had come a long way since first researching my previous *Promotable Woman* video and book projects 20 years ago. Not wanting to trust my instincts alone, I asked other women what they thought. I found that they too had mixed feelings.

Success is taking the potential you were born with and living up to it!

Dr. Jan Northup

When I asked friend and colleague, Eydie Hiebert, if she thought we had come a long way, she was not hesitant in replying. Eydie knows about the ups and downs of making a mark in retail business management, an area that had previously been a male-only possibility. For twenty-nine years she has worked to bring women recognition as professional contributors to retail. She shares her journey and thoughts:

The Company Girl

Why do some people pick certain careers? Relationships? Why do we pick the most traveled road? Or the one without a footprint? I only know that as a child every day was a glorious one, filled with the freedom to do and be whatever I imagined I could be.

Raised in the backcountry of Manitoba, Canada, I plotted my path hourly. I dreamed of being and doing. I ran free on our small farm, far from any city with their large institutions and throngs of busy people; an oasis without rules and regulations, completely unrestricted. Of course, there weren't many options for getting into trouble; but I did succeed on many occasions!

I had always dreamed of being a teacher, but when I look back now I can see my predetermined career and life path …

It all started with color: green trees, green grass, pink and purple flowers blowing in the wind, light blue skies and fluffy white clouds, orange butterflies, yellow bumble bees and the soft color of a newborn calf, puppy or lamb. Maybe it was all of these things that attracted me to retail and started my career. The large department store was full of merchandise of every size, color and description that I could never have dreamed of in the drab environment of poverty.

My first introduction to a telex machine, a combo, managing a sales team in customer service and then … merchandising!!! These were just the tools to get my hands on those racks of color. Although I thought my forte seemed to be bossing people around, I was told that I was a born manager. Being a multitasker and highly organized individual, these two abilities were the only tools I had to train myself in the business of selling and marketing.

One more powerful part of my being was paranoia. I lived in fear of losing my job.

In a world where women did not rise to the top, could I not in fact climb that nonexistent career ladder? These were the days of the old boys clubs, when narrow high-heeled shoes were the only available ones for purchase and the dress code for women was, "Please, skirts and dresses only." Because the good old boys did realize that with a ladder for us to climb, the view for them would have been much better.

Now we have a "ladder," and wouldn't you know it, all the "company girls" wriggled to the top, only to find the old boys laughing as we hit the solid glass ceiling. We fought and struggled to gain recognition and found tools to break through the glass. The few who did get through, thankfully, were able to eke more of us through when all of a sudden, the jet-age plastic – Plexiglas – replaced the breakable barrier.

But, being a company girl, I took everything I was told to be gospel. Being of a naïve nature, I was the target of many jokes and was regarded as somewhat of an ignoramus. I didn't know gross profit from dirty puddin'.

My markdown books and laundry sheets stayed in pristine condition on their shelves for the first 6 months. I didn't understand what their purpose was, but lo and behold, one day I was called into the office of the assistant manager. I was congratulated on the awesome gross profit that had been produced in my departments. One of the more memorable experiences for being put "on the carpet" vertically.

So with a lot of "little moments" from my direct supervisor, I slowly learned the retail business. My manager was very patient and vowed to turn me into a businesswoman. I was the only department manager at that location to recognize the experience and knowledge of this man. He helped me daily in my quest to understand how to do my job, how to excel, how to dress, and how to market the merchandise in the departments in my charge.

He instilled in me pride and a desire to learn. He also opened the door to many opportunities I would never have had. His faith in me has allowed me to believe in myself and stay true to my convictions. At this point in his career he was focused on people. He truly cared and wanted me to succeed. I will always remember this man for his belief in me and for his patience and support.

Now, with a bit of knowledge and a lot of persistence and perseverance I was a tyrant in the making!

But, try as they might, not one of my superiors could entice me to take up the "politics of retail," and there were many … all male … for 25 years!

The pink-collar trade, and not one of them knew how to motivate one backwards girl from Boggy Creek, Manitoba.

I did have a co-worker who was educated and raised in Ontario. She had traveled the world and read voraciously, as did I. That led me in a direction of self-learning. Steering me on course, I started my style of educating myself. I took courses on anything that interested me. I read business magazines and traded the Calgary Sun *for* The Globe and Mail. *It wasn't all books and reading. I learned how to swim at age 34 and learned how to downhill ski at age 38!*

I learned a great deal more from my children as they progressed through school. I learned about people. I learned about faith, love, and the deep, deep roots of family. I learned of loss, empty nests, and pride as I watched my children take flight. From them came strength; the strength to say, "Hey, I am worth something, I do have intelligence, I can do anything I set my mind to."

I even knew the answer to the question." How does God make rocks?"

But, I could not and did not want to pay the price for entrance into the crystal palace. I watched and waited as other women slithered through the cracks and disintegrated in the process. Prostitution is not only on the street corners, that trade can be plied anywhere, anytime. With the usual outcome – and it ain't in your pocket, baby!

I ask you, girl ... for this I burned my bra???

For every Sinead, Greer or Jolie out there ... five thousand Brittany's keep knocking us back to the 1800s. The only difference is more skin! With a plump underbelly designed by the new and increasing number of plastic surgeons, pardon me, cosmetic surgeons, plastic is so passé ... although the entire breast is now encased in plastic and saline ...

So ... have we come a long way baby? Or has our goal of the '60s been obliterated by the babes who still believe blonde, boobs, bias, and gimme, gimme at an accelerated speed is now our inheritance? As women, we must realize naturally by nurturing, we are the leaders of that generation of women that we sought to be. We must continue to underline, redirect, and redesign, so our daughters, our sons and grandchildren understand that our earth and the people in it are truly the fabric that will lead to peace and prosperity for everyone.

So baby, get with it. We got a long way to go ... the journey is never over ... the road is just in need of repair.

So, I thought the next step would be to look for research studies that would resolve the question. Once again, there were mixed messages, or should I call them interpretations of research findings? The gap that previously existed between men and women in the workplace has narrowed and single women are no longer exclusively the heads of the household and the primary care giver to children and elderly dependents. More men in our society are the primary care giver to their children and their elderly parents, relatives and friends. But questions still loom and are asked of me as I travel throughout the United States and abroad:

1. Can women in our society successfully pursue a career, realize their passions for a cause and balance those with the roles of wife, significant other, mother, daughter, sister, friend, neighbor and community member?
2. Why do some women seem to be successful and others seem to experience failure and rejection?
3. Can women find personal and professional success in what is still a male-dominated society?
4. Are women receiving equal pay for equal work?

5. Are women accepted in nontraditional jobs and careers or are they met with "this is no job for a woman"?

6. And finally, Have we come a long way baby or do we still have a long way to go?

My early experience and my experience today tell me that we still have a long way to go, baby.

So, to set the stage for the upcoming chapters, the following general statistics are presented. I know statistics can be manipulated or presented in a way that will support any idea or conclusion, but what I am going to present here and throughout the book are statistics or data from sources that are recognized as reliable at the time of writing this book. There are so many variables that can impact how data about women are reported that I challenge you to research and follow the statistics or data that relate to your unique situation, career field or other influencing factors. This will give you first-hand knowledge that you can use in your own career decisions. Other findings will be presented in later chapters as they relate to the specific topic being discussed. By the end of the book you can decide if you have come a long way or if you still have a long way to go.

Wage Gap Over Time

The most commonly quoted statistic is in the area of wage differences between women and men. According to the U.S. Census Bureau, the following was reported as the per dollar earnings for women compared to men from 1995 through 2005:

Year	Earnings (cents per dollar)
1995	71.4
1996	73.8
1997	74.2
1998	73.2
1999	72.3
2000	73.7
2001	76.3
2002	76.6
2003	75.5
2004	76.6
2005	77.0

It is interesting to note that in 1963 the Equal Pay Act was signed into law by the U.S. Congress. It was written to eliminate the discrepancy between wages paid to women and men performing the same job or duties within an organization. The following chart demonstrates a wage gap by gender and race, based on median annual earnings of white men, was reported by the U.S. Population Survey and the National Committee on Pay Equity.

There is a gap within the male population groups but a larger gap between women and their male counterparts. In 1985, when The Promotable Woman: What Makes the Difference was released, women as a collective group were earning 57.4 cents for every dollar earned by men. It doesn't take a math degree to realize that we seem to be on a slow boat to the $1.00 for $1.00 equity bank!

Year	White	Black men	Hispanic	White	Black women	Hispanic
1970	100%	69.0%	n.a.	58.7%	48.2%	n.a.
1975	100	74.3	72.1%	57.5	55.4	49.3%
1980	100	70.7	70.8	58.9	55.7	50.5
1985	100	69.7	68.0	63.0	57.1	52.1
1990	100	73.1	66.3	69.4	62.5	54.3
1992	100	72.6	63.3	70.0	64.0	55.4
1994	100	75.1	64.3	71.6	63.0	55.6
1995	100	75.9	63.3	71.2	64.2	53.4
1996	100	80.0	63.9	73.3	65.1	56.6
1997	100	75.1	61.4	71.9	62.6	53.9
1998	100	74.9	61.6	72.6	62.6	53.1
1999	100	80.6	61.6	71.6	65.0	52.1
2000	100	78.2	63.4	72.2	64.6	52.8
2003	100	78.2	63.3	75.6	65.4	54.3
2004	100	74.5	63.2	76.7	68.4	56.9

Madam Speaker

In 1917, three years before women were guaranteed the constitutional right to vote, Jean Rankin of Montana became the first woman to be elected to Congress. Ninety years later, Democrat Nancy Pelosi of California became the first woman speaker of the U.S. House of Representatives. In 1997, Madeleine Albright was the sixty-fourth and first female Secretary of State. More and more women are entering politics and making their voice heard on important issues facing our nation. Historically, the number of opportunities for women to reach Congress has been limited; partly due to the fact that the incumbents were men and most incumbents win re-election and voters have not seen women as major players in politics. Recent elections have shown that women are serious opponents in political races at the local, state and national levels. Today, women hold 70 of the 435 seats in the House of Representative and 14 seats in the Senate. With only one women on the nine member U.S. Supreme Court and only one on the eighteen member Senate Judiciary Committee, nine women governors and eleven lieutenant governors, there is still work to be done to have a more gender-balanced government.

A World View

The Gender Gap Index 2006: A New Framework for Measuring Equality published by the World Economic Forum was the result of collaboration with the faculty at Harvard University and London Business School. The purpose was to evaluate gender gaps of 115 countries (nations) in four primary areas: economic participation and opportunity, educational attainment, health and survival and political empowerment. In summary, the overall ranking of the United States (23) lags behind many European nations and Canada (14). Canada shows a more consistent performance, ranking well on two categories – economic participation and opportunity (10) and educational attainment (21) – and less so on the other two – political empowerment (33) and health and survival (51). The United States' ranking on economic participation and opportunity (3), educational attainment (66), political empowerment (66) and sharing a one ranking with 33 other countries on health and survival indicates that women in the United States fare well in comparison to other countries in some areas, but, surprisingly, they lag in others. Considering all four factors evaluated, the following in order of ranking (1-10) are Sweden, Norway, Finland, Iceland, Germany, Philippines, New Zealand, Denmark, United Kingdom and Ireland. What does this mean? It means that as a group, women need to continue using the successes and initiatives women in other countries have, look at our own initiatives and determine what strategies or practices are positively influencing their equality.

From Past to Present

Whether we are talking about government or business leadership, women around the world have and are making a difference. In developing The Promotable Woman: What Makes the Difference video training program, we asked men and women in various occupations and job levels what had made the difference for them in achieving success. What skills made the difference? What advice? What attitudes? What obstacles? What person? Did they have a role model or a mentor? We found that the skills and attitudes necessary for success are universal. They apply to everyone, women and men alike. In addition to the universal skills and attitudes necessary for achieving success, women in our society still have special needs or concerns. These concerns include balancing career and home responsibilities, finding mentors, and pursuing uninterrupted education and training programs. These concerns are experienced less frequently by men.

The Chicken or the Egg?

Before we go on, I want to talk about your ability to achieve success as it relates to your beliefs about where success comes from and whether you are in a position to embrace the success that is possible for you. The debate among psychologists and others as to whether the success instinct is inborn or whether it is a product of environment and learning has endured for years – it is known as the nature-nurture controversy. In other words, are you born with the drive to succeed, to achieve your goals and achieve satisfaction in what you do (nature) or do you develop this drive through your learning experiences and the messages that you hear from others (nurture)?

One article, book or speaker assures us with data and examples as to how nature is the sole determinant of our current situation and our future outcome. The next article, book or speaker convinces us, again with data and examples, as to how nurture determines our current status and future outcome. I am sure the debate will continue. Does it have to be one or the other? Is there only black and white? And why is it that two siblings, even twins with the same genetic makeup and environmental conditions, take totally different approaches to life and whose successes, or lack of them, are totally different? Do we really have to know if the chicken or the egg came first, so to speak? I don't think so.

The nature versus nurture debate has been impacted by the speed at which our personal and professional needs have changed and seem to keep on changing. At one time it was believed that a person's values were formed between three and seven years after birth. Those values basically stayed the same throughout the person's life unless an experience was so critical or significant (positive or negative) that it brought about a change in the way they viewed the world around them. Let me give you a few examples of critical or significant events. You can then determine whether any of these events were catalysts for changing how you viewed the world around you.

- Extremely good health – health problems
- Marriage – divorce
- Birth of a child – loss of a child
- Success in school – difficulty in school
- Good physical appearance – poor physical appearance

Whether from inborn traits (nature) or from environmental experiences (nurture) or a combination, each of you has his or her own attitudes (definition) about what it means to be successful. Viewing the world around you includes how you view yourself and how you evaluate your own success or failure in your world. Who you are today and what your future holds for you must surely be a combination of your nature instilled tendencies and a synthesis of your nurturing experiences, learnings, past successes and failures. I also think your ability to experience success depends on your willingness to explore the factors that have been identified as vital to finding success in jobs, relationships and your general attitude about life. Those who are successful are those who are willing and open to new ways of thinking and doing.

In the following chapters, we will explore the factors that have made a difference in the lives of successful people and, specifically, successful women. You will have the opportunity to examine strategies and techniques that have worked for others and examine how to apply them to your own life.

We all have experienced obstacles, disappointments, and setbacks in our personal and our professional lives. These obstacles have either interrupted our productivity and momentum or they have served as a catalyst to propel us positively in a new direction. As the Asian saying goes, "An enemy can be as useful as a Buddha," which means an obstacle can be as useful as an opportunity if it motivates and challenges you. It all depends on how you view the obstacle and how you view life's challenges.

Several strategies will be presented that make a difference in maneuvering around any obstacles that you think you will encounter. This is not a list of do's and don'ts, but strategies that you can use every day, both personally and professionally. You will come to recognize and put into use specific techniques that direct your attention away from obstacles, techniques that make use of your past positive experiences to ensure future success.

This book should serve as a resource guide. It can be used to examine your personal wants and desires as well as to help you establish a career blueprint. Although each of the following chapters stands alone, it is recommended that you complete them in sequence for maximum benefit.

Prosperity Thinking. Prosperity Thinking is knowing that there is an abundance in all aspects of our lives and being able to visualize and experience that abundance. Remember Robert Louis Stevenson's quote: "The world is so full of a number of things, I am sure we should all be happy as kings." Abundance is a natural state.

Patterns for Power. In Patterns for Power you will gain a better understanding of your personal pattern or style of working with others. You will learn the communication skills necessary to be in control of your life.

Positioning. Positioning demonstrates how to surround yourself with an environment for success and with the skills and people who bring out the best in you. It will show you how to form relationships with people who multiply your efforts for mutual benefit. You will have the opportunity to examine your personal beliefs about your multiple roles and responsibilities and the pros and cons of trying to do it all.

Prescriptions for Comfort Management. In Prescriptions for Comfort Management we will explore strategies that enable you to transform stress management into comfort management. An overview of several comfort management techniques will be given. It will be up to you to choose the technique most compatible with your lifestyle.

Programming for Play. As adults we've forgotten the therapeutic value of play. In Programming for Play, you will explore and select a physical activity that is fun and compatible with your individual style. We will be talking about two particular health conditions pertinent to women and how they make a difference in our lives and overall on-the-job performance.

Principal and Interest. Principal and Interest is about money. You will have an opportunity to examine techniques that will help you focus on achieving financial abundance. Money is important because it provides the resources necessary for your lifetime development. We will discuss techniques for establishing an image that sends a positive and professional message.

Purposing. A leading authority on management coined the word Purposing, which means purpose and action. It's simply making a wish with a due date, otherwise know as goal setting. Each of you will have the opportunity to set your personal and professional goals to empower you to live up to your fullest potential.

Finally, this book is a resource of ideas, examples and strategies to allow you to get the success that you envision for yourself. Success is not the life that someone else has designed, but living the life that you want and need. The trick is to practice and reinforce the factors that lead to success. The following are success factors over which you have control:

- Moving from knowing to doing
- Closing the gap between dreaming or visioning to goal achievement
- Shedding expectations of others and owning your own expectations
- Adopting a positive attitude toward change
- Accepting your limitations and celebrating your strengths
- Developing communication skills that effectively tell others who you really are
- Forming alliances that support your goals
- Maintaining emotional, physical and psychological health

Choices We Make

Each chapter begins with a self-assessment that will give you insight into your perception of your personal and professional life. Insights are wonderful, but you must DO something about what you've learned. You will choose the actions that you think will give you the best results. Does anyone make every choice/decision perfectly? I don't think so. Every choice we make impacts the next choice, which impacts the next choice, which impacts the next choice and so on. You get my point.

Every choice we make, whether the right or best choice or the wrong or worst choice, will impact the next point at which we need to make a choice or decision about what to say, what to do, how to react, or what not to say, what not to do or how not to react. If you have no reason to change the

*Insanity
(a definition):
Doing the same thing
over and over again
and expecting different
results.*

Albert Einstein

direction of your life, you are in a great place. If you are not in a great place, let me repeat, insights are wonderful, but you must do something about what you've learned. Otherwise, everything stays the same.

People who report the best results in making changes are those who practice newly learned concepts until they become internalized. In his original book *Psycho-cybernetics*, (and the latest *Psycho-cybernetics for a New Millennium*), Maxwell Maltz suggests that it takes a minimum of twenty-one days of practice to change or develop an attitude, habit or behavior.

You Are One Of A Kind

The most important thing to remember is that you are an individual and that different ideas will impact different people in different ways. This book is yours to explore in such a way that it will make a difference in how you move forward in your personal and professional life. Reinforcement activities at the end of each chapter will allow you to internalize and apply the concepts presented.

Chapter 1
Prosperity Thinking

SELF-ASSESSMENT

Before reading this chapter, rate yourself on the questions listed below.

How comfortable are you with your success?

Not at all _____Very

How often do you recall negative events in your past?

Not at all_____Often

How well have you been able to focus your thoughts and energies on positive outcomes?

Not at all _____Very well

To what degree have you been able to get rid of your fear of failure?

Not at all _____Completely

How committed are you to your goals?

Not at all _____Very

Prosperity Thinking

*Whether you believe you can do a thing or
believe you can't,
you are right.*

Henry Ford

Prosperity Thinking is the attitude that makes the difference! It is knowing that there is an abundance of wealth available to you in all aspects of your life. Wealth is not just money; it is warmth and safety and privacy and comfort. It is opportunity and freedom from want or fear. It is ease and luxury and opportunities for advancement. Some women tend to think that love, happiness, career opportunities and money can only come from one source. This way of thinking is limiting the universe in ways that it can provide for you. Love, happiness, career opportunities and money are available in abundance and from many sources. Knowing that this abundance is available to us and truly believing that we are deserving of it is Prosperity Thinking. That's the tricky part, truly believing that we are deserving of that abundance. Not realizing the abundance and not thinking of ourselves as deserving are learned attitudes. If these attitudes are limiting you, they should be relearned.

Whether we realize it or not, we carry on internal conversations all day long. We talk to ourselves at 800-1000 words per minute. This inner self-talk can be positive and supportive or negative and self-limiting. It interprets the events and circumstances that we encounter. It determines whether we are rich or poor, powerful or weak, happy or unhappy. Our inner self-talk is a powerful shaper of our life. We need to become fully aware of the force and power of these internal messages.

Instead of seeing obstacles as problems or setbacks, learn to see them as challenges, learning experiences, or opportunities. Reinforce this new awareness by taking the words problem, obstacle or any other self-limiting word out of your vocabulary. Whenever you use self-limiting words you lose a sense of control. So, every time you start to say problem or obstacle, substitute a word that will put you in charge of your environment.

We are going to spend time focusing our attention on positive experiences in the past and in the imagined future. Every person accomplishes success at some point in life. Success is readily apparent when we feel good about something we have done or when others note our accomplishments. As infants, we were rewarded for the smallest act. I can remember how my husband and I rewarded our son with smiles and oohs and aahs of approval the first time he smiled, even though my mother reminded me that he was probably just having gas pains. His first word, his first steps were reinforced by our hugs, our cheers, and our laughter.

As children, we quickly learned what would bring positive feedback from those around us. But, as we matured, accomplishments became more complex. Goals were set by society, our educational system, or our employer; and we were rewarded by a known, anticipated event such as graduation or a paycheck.

Take The Plunge

As adults, the process of achieving success is not as well-defined. We have the freedom to define our own successes as well as our failures. Some people are very good at defining and acknowledging their own accomplishments. These people tend to appear successful because they feel successful. They are content with the direction their lives are taking one minute and are impatient to experience even more highs. They practice Prosperity Thinking and experience the incredible emotions that come with it. My favorite image of Prosperity Thinking and the feelings and emotions related to it is the "Nestea plunge." A frequently seen TV ad shows a person standing at the edge of a swimming pool with arms outstretched. Then they just fall backwards into the pool in a relaxed movement of total freedom, trusting that they will soon be surrounded by the wonderfully refreshing water below. Another image I like is the "Toyota kick." Although the less flexible I become, the less likely I am to attempt it. On the TV ad, a person jumps into the air and clicks both feet together. Leaping into the air, there is an unspoken message that they will land on their feet. Such a coordinated display of the uninhibited expression of positive emotions!

This concentration on the positive is a key to success. It's what sets the successful apart from the unsuccessful. There are specific techniques that can be learned and practiced that will enable you to employ positive focusing as an everyday habit, techniques that will allow you to achieve personal and professional abundance.

The ability to focus on the positive is directly related to our ability to extrapolate positive experiences from our past. The process of remembering is very selective, but you are the selector. If you habitually remember negative events, you will reexperience memories that leave you angry, frustrated, helpless or depressed. Some people develop this behavior as a habit. They receive attention, reinforcement, or emotional and psychological rewards for continuing to focus on the negative aspects of their past. This habit may have come from early programming that has never been counteracted with internal or external positive reinforcement. On the other hand, if you habitually remember positive events, you will reexperience and magnify quality memories that leave you feeling calm, happy, confident and successful.

Believing that success is possible for you rests on the evidence that you have experienced positive events before and, therefore, you can experience them again. We can't

5

live without experiencing some successful events. So if you hear yourself or someone else saying *"life's a bitch,"* then you know that many positive events are being ignored or denied.

We can learn to change the way we view ourselves. One way is by consciously recalling events in our lives of which we can be proud. Events do not have to be major benchmarks; they can be small, everyday occurrences that made us feel good.

This means you must focus your attention more on positive events in the past and positive expectations in your imagined future. If you reflect on your life, you may discover that the more you expected certain positive outcomes, the easier it was for you to take the action that created that outcome.

Higher expectations lead to motivation, greater motivation leads to success.

No one ever attained success by focusing on failure. We can never accomplish anything that we think of as impossible or undeserved. This means that if you completely believe, consciously and subconsciously, that something is impossible or undeserved, then it is impossible for you. Think of yourself as being deserving and you will begin experiencing abundance. If you are interested in living an abundant life, you must stop repeating internal negative programming. Remember, negative programming was learned from past negative experiences.

The three-step antidote for any self-imposed limitations that you might have is:

Watch your thoughts; they become words. Watch your words; they become actions. Watch your actions; they become habits. Watch your habits; they become character. Watch your character; it becomes your destiny.

Author Unknown

1. Bring the limiting thoughts and feelings to the surface.
2. Examine the limiting thoughts.
3. Make the decision to turn limiting thoughts and feelings into Prosperity Thinking.

You have the ability to change all or any part of these damaging messages. According to the 19th century philosopher William James, the greatest discovery of his generation was that human beings, by changing the inner attitudes of their minds, could change the outer aspects of their lives. James' generation had only rediscovered that principle. Marcus Aurelius, Roman Emperor 121-180 A.D., said "Your life is what your thoughts make it. If you can change your thoughts, you can change your life." And from the Bible, "As a man thinketh in his heart, so is he." What each was referring to was the ability to *visualize* through the use of mental pictures, relaxation and an internal focusing on a desired outcome.

At the end of this chapter you will learn an activity that will allow you to correct any negative self-talk by replacing it with new, positive self-talk messages. To do this we will use a technique that is the key to Prosperity Thinking, one that will be used throughout this book. This technique is the Posture of Excellence. The *Posture of Excellence* incorporates visualization – the ability to change your thoughts on a subconscious level.

The mind has a remarkable power to visualize, to actually see pictures, faces, and places in our mind's eye.

The mind has the ability to see a desired condition as if it's real. Unfortunately, most of us do not harness this power to help us succeed. We tend to use this power negatively, to reinforce failure. Every time we worry, we envision the worst. We experience fear thoughts. But it is just as easy to use this power to envision success, happiness, financial abundance and career advancement.

Visualization has been used throughout history in many disciplines, and most recently by sport psychologists in working with Olympic and professional athletes. The publicity surrounding its effectiveness in athletic training has added new credibility to visualization. It has taken the technique out of the mysterious, mystical, touchy-feely and even feminine arena and has transformed visualization into a legitimate skill that can be learned and practiced. The sports-training model includes the following techniques:

1. Learn to relax quickly. In a relaxed state you can reach beyond the conscious mind.
2. Stage repeated mental rehearsals. Visualize the desired outcome as if it has already happened.
3. Use positive self-talk to turn negative thoughts and fears into positive action. Obviously athletes visualize winning!

Going For The Gold

I have had the pleasure of meeting and getting to know two-time Olympian Lindsay Alcock. Lindsay represents a new generation of strong Canadian women and role models. Her perspective, earned through years of competing on icy tracks around the world, draws poignant parallels between sports and business that have inspired many individuals in the corporate community. She shares her thoughts on the power of visualization:

In preparation for the 2006 Olympic Winter Games in Turin, Italy, it was essential that I visualized my Skeleton race months in advance. How is it possible to re-create the feeling of sliding at 80 mph on my stomach on a steel sled, with my chin only inches from the ice? With the exception of the incredible G-force we feel going through the icy curves, it is completely realistic to mimic a run down the Olympic track. I had already taken sixteen runs down the challenging 19-curve track in the year prior. I had a pretty good idea about what areas I needed to work on to be the fastest athlete in the field of fifteen Olympic competitors. What is amazing is that I had the power to take another fifty runs down the track through the use of proper visualization techniques in the weeks leading up to the race.

Months before the Olympics, I was falling asleep at night thinking about the Turin track and waking up slightly startled because I was fearful that I had missed something important that day. When I saw an Olympic commercial on TV, my heart rate quickened and goose bumps overtook my body. It didn't matter that this was my second Olympics – the anxiety and excitement were coming on just as intensely as my first experience in Salt Lake City, Utah in 2002 where I placed 6th. I just knew that there was a real shot at getting on the podium at these Olympics.

My visualization began early in the season by pasting large photos of the Turin start and finish sliding areas in my journal. I often diarize my travel and race experiences while I am on the Skeleton World Cup

9

tour. Every time I opened my journal, I saw the exact same image that I would see on race day in Turin: the start block, the glistening ice, the angle of the slope down to curve one, and the spectator stands track-side. It was essential that my brain became accustomed with this sight. The finish area picture was pasted in the back of the journal as a way to help me imagine the celebration and the incredible feeling of elation that I would feel coming up the braking stretch. I WANTED to see the #1 flash on the finish clock. These two photos would positively enhance my visualization techniques.

About two weeks prior to my departure to Italy for the Olympics, my coach and I planned a pre-Olympic camp in beautiful Canmore, Alberta in the Rocky Mountains. It was a special three-day commitment during which I would focus solely on quality high-intensity physical training and take part in intensive visualization sessions without distractions from the outside world. My coach and I were having a high-performance retreat to finalize the strategy for the biggest race of my life.

During the visualization sessions, I placed my sled down on the hotel room floor and set up my laptop computer with the screen close to my face, at eye level. To help me remember the course, I played video footage of the Turin curves from the vantage point of what the slider sees at real speed. I began to carry out the same body movements involved with steering a sled: the shifting of body weight, pushing in the knees and shoulders, and executing small head steers just like I would do on the actual track.

For the second run, I would close my eyes and imagine the same run using only my sensory perceptions. I saw the curves coming at me at real speeds, I heard the roar of the crowd as I whooshed by them and I felt my muscles contract as I executed the same steers all the way down to the finish line. To make things more fun, my coach would time me with a watch to see if my visualizing matched the same relative run time of sixty seconds to get down the Turin track.

Once I had done the work, I could then allow myself a moment to visualize the best part – the celebration of winning a medal. I have been able to recall past sporting achievements when emotions completely took over my body and I was hysterically jumping up and down. By substituting that feeling of past elation into my new visualization (minus the act of jumping up and down!), I could imagine actually feeling that in the Olympic race.

It was astonishing to see the physiological effects that came over me immediately following the intense visualization sessions. My heart rate was rapid and I had to take a moment to catch my breath. My coach even described how glassy my eyes appeared. Through mastering the visualization technique and imagery, I managed to replicate the same physical feeling that I would typically get sliding down the real ice track. My body's nervous system had been put through a mini-workout, which is why daily sessions should last no longer than fifteen minutes. Try to stop the mind after the session through the use of distractions such as reading a book, watching TV, or listening to music.

*Visualization is about capturing quality imagery over quantity. With that in mind, you must always be alert prior to one of these sessions. If your body and mind are tired, you won't get the same vividness in your imagery. It is so important to do the work first before you imagine the elation and euphoria of the positive outcome. Always visualize **positive** things happening to you. If, for some reason, you imagined an adverse outcome or conjured up a negative feeling, stop what you are doing and take a break from the whole process. You can come back to the exercise with a clearer mind and get back to imagining yourself achieving incredible things.*

I finished 10th overall in the 2006 Olympic Skeleton race but I had achieved a new level of visualization that had exceeded my expectations and that had helped me to mentally prepare for a challenging test. I had tapped into something very powerful and I will continue to practice these skills as I get closer to the 2010 Olympic Winter Games in Vancouver and Whistler, Canada.

Oh, Where Oh Where Did My Rose Colored Glasses Go?

You don't need rose colored glasses; you don't need any glasses. You simply need to learn a new way of seeing.

When seminar participants have told me that they couldn't visualize, I asked them if they would be able to find their car in the parking lot when they left. Amused, they replied, "Of course!" If you can close your eyes and imagine what your car looks like, then you have the ability to visualize. If you are not convinced that you have the ability to visualize, close your eyes and try **not** to see a pink elephant with purple polka-dots. Some people actually see pictures in their mind. Some people may get a feeling, not an actual picture. They only sense the image or outcome on which they are focusing; that is still visualization.

It should be obvious now that whatever you focus your attention on grows stronger. The more you focus your attention on positive events in your past, the more evidence you will have to expect positive events in your future. Seeing our unlimited possibilities is exhilarating.

An activity that I used with junior high students to make this point was to have them to look down at the floor, frown and repeat with me the words happy, excited, exhilarating, successful, friendly, outgoing and loveable. Usually after only a few words they would begin smiling and giggling. I would then ask them to look up toward the ceiling, smile and repeat with me words like angry, depressed, upset, frustrated, rejected, alone and sad. Nods of understanding would soon be apparent. You see, you cannot hold two thoughts simultaneously. You can think happy and then you can think sad immediately afterward, but you cannot think both thoughts at the same time. I have used this same activity with thousands of adults around the world and the response has been the same. Even though the concept seems so simple, how many of us have ever really thought about it? How many of us have used this inability to hold two thoughts simultaneously to our advantage in our personal or professional interactions or to gain a sense of control over our environment?

We all have had commitments that we really did not want to fulfill, such as going to a mandatory training, a business meeting or a family dinner. You knew the speaker would be boring, you knew the meeting was going to be a rehash of the same old issues and, as usual, Uncle Fred would yell at Uncle Bill as they had done for 20 years. Sure enough, you were right.

On a different occasion you decided that you would give the speaker the benefit of doubt. You would learn at least one piece of new information at the meeting and you wouldn't let Uncle Fred and Uncle Bill bother you. After all,

The ancestor of every action is a thought.

Ralph Waldo Emerson

they will still be yelling at each other for another 20 years – that's just what they do. You used positive self-talk to turn a negative situation into one that was not only tolerable but positive. You and you alone changed the outcome of the situation.

Do you ever find yourself recalling or repeating a particularly negative past experience when you felt unsuccessful, one that affected your self-image then and continues to shape your self-image today? Perhaps it was a disagreement with another person that was not resolved, an embarrassing situation, a time when you tried something new and it flopped. Take time to think about that. Do you still replay the situation in your mind today, carrying on artificial dialogues with several possible endings? Do you see yourself in that embarrassing situation and try to replay the ending so that you aren't embarrassed? Or do you replay that disagreement, only this time standing up to the person and giving them a piece of your mind, or perhaps taking back or softening the words that you used. Of course you've done this, we all have. It is only natural to protect our self-esteem, our ego, so we keep replaying old memories hoping to resolve them to our ego's satisfaction.

To counteract and bring you out of negative feelings, I am going to show you what I call the Posture of Excellence. This exercise involves having you picture yourself in a past situation in which you were in an optimal performance mode, feeling very resourceful or excellent, getting the desired results. It's not just physically standing tall, but a mental posture as well as, a feeling of excellence. To attain this posture you should close your eyes and relax. It is a good idea to find a quiet place where you will not be interrupted. Sit comfortably in a chair or lie on the floor or on your bed. Play some soft music in the background. Music without words, preferably classical or new-age music with a slow beat, has been found to be an effective aid in helping the body relax. If you play popular music, there is a tendency to be distracted by associative memories or singing along with the words. When you are deeply relaxed you are in touch with your subconscious.

Now, recall a time when you were feeling resourceful and excellent. Be aware of thoughts and feelings when you recall that event. Then select a word or phrase that best describes that state. You'll use that word as your CUE WORD or CUE PHRASE. In the future, this word or phrase will act as a prompt to help you replace any negative feelings with the preferred Posture of Excellence. Your cue word could be the name of a person who inspires you, a place of serenity or adventure, or a feeling related to an accomplishment.

Choosing your cue word or phrase is simple; in fact, it is like buying a pair of shoes. Have you ever walked into the shoe department, seen a pair of shoes and said. "That's my pair of shoes!" You tried them on, they looked great; they felt good; and then you wore them the next day and they killed your feet! Or on a different day, you saw a different pair of shoes and said, "That's my pair of shoes!" You tried them on, they looked great; they felt good; and then you wore them until they practically fell off your feet. And someone is going to have to sneak into your closet in the dark of night and throw them away so you don't wear them in public anymore. Or still another day, there was another pair of shoes that you saw and said, "That's my pair of shoes!" They were a silver metallic that would match perfectly the dress you bought for the dinner dance. You tried them on, they looked great; they felt good; and you wore them to the dance. You only wore them once, but they were perfect for that occasion.

Remember, "try on" several cue words until you find one that "fits." Your cue word may change and evolve over time as you change and evolve. Most people have a standard cue word or phrase that they use most of the time, but, occasionally they need a special cue word or phrase for a special situation.

I have used the same cue phrase for almost 30 years. That phrase is "I am calm." In almost any stressful situation I can regain control or refocus my attention by using this phrase. There are times, however, when I do not want to be calm. There are times when I need to energize myself. Just before I speak before an audience – be it thirty or three hundred – I smile and say "I am happy and excited to have the opportunity to be here!" or I enthusiastically reaffirm "I love what I do!"

Repeat your cue word silently several times a day so that it becomes natural to you. Then, whenever you want to adopt the preferred stance – your Posture of Excellence – when in a stressful situation or when you need something on which to build confidence, simply recall and repeat your cue word or phrase. That will allow you to replace any negative thoughts and feelings with your Posture of Excellence.

As soon as you find yourself in a nonexcellent posture, recalling past events that have not been resolved to your satisfaction or responding to negativity in your current environment, you can repeat your cue word or phrase to trigger an excellent posture. This exercise is based on the principle that one emotion counteracts another and that you cannot hold two thoughts simultaneously.

I am not suggesting that you ignore or deny that you have had negative experiences in your past. Who you are today is a combination of all of your past experiences – both positive and negative. But if recalling any past negative experiences is interrupting your on-the-job performance or negatively impacting your personal relationships, then you must employ strategies to counteract them. The following Practice Application will allow you to employ the Posture of Excellence to counteract any event or person that is impacting negatively on you.

Practice Application

Read the instructions through completely so that you understand the practice application process. After you have done that, spend a few minutes completing the activity. To practice the Posture of Excellence:

- Get into a comfortable position with music playing softly in the background.
- Close your eyes.
- Take several deep breaths as you relax with the music.
- Inhale deeply through your nose and gently exhale through you mouth as if gently blowing out a candle. Take several deep breaths as you relax with the music. Repeat this several times and then just breathe normally.
- Recall a time when you were at peak performance. With your eyes still closed, recall those feelings of success, confidence, accomplishment and pride. See in your mind the posture of your body, note your facial expression, feel the energy and exuberance, and hear the praise and support from friends and colleagues.
- As you are relaxed, listening to soft music, you can practice replacing old negative programming with genuine positive programming about a successful, confident you. With your eyes closed, take several deep breaths and let your mind wander. Remember a happy time or many happy times. These times often are centered around joyful experiences as an individual, such as when you learned something new or when were in a satisfying relationship. Picture yourself warm, satisfied, safe, secure, unhurried, joyful and abundant.

- See in your mind the posture of your body, note your facial expression. What word or phrase comes to mind as you recall this happy time?
- Think of a time when you successfully accomplished something as an individual: learning to ride a bicycle, receiving compliments on a job-related task, or any event that still reminds you of your accomplishments.
- Feel the energy and exuberance and hear the praise and support from friends and colleagues. What word or phrase comes to mind as you recall a time of accomplishment?
- Again, see in your mind the posture of your body and note your facial expression.
- Observe your feelings, thoughts and energy level before you begin the Posture of Excellence activity and after you finish it.
- Focus on memories that are most fulfilling and supportive to your sense of self-worth and, as the music continues, repeat these or similar affirmations:
  - ❖ *I am deserving of the abundance of the world.*
  - ❖ *I am deserving of love.*
  - ❖ *I am deserving of my past accomplishments.*
  - ❖ *I am worthy of ease and luxury.*
  - ❖ *I am worthy of opportunity.*
  - ❖ *I am worthy of warmth and safety.*
  - ❖ *I am worthy of happiness.*
  - ❖ *A Promotable Woman wears a Posture of Excellence.*

> ❖ *I wear a Posture of Excellence.*
> ❖ *I am a Promotable Woman.*

- Remain relaxed with your eyes closed as you continue feeling good about your successes. Then, whenever you are ready, slowly stretch your arms and legs, feeling energized and wide awake with renewed vitality.

This practice should be done each day for a week or more. When you are first learning and practicing the Posture of Excellence activity, it is a good idea to practice in the same place and at the same time every day. In that way, you will internalize your Posture of Excellence and it will be available as a resource whenever you need it.

Reinforcement Activities

1. To make you strong for the future, have numerous positive memories available to counteract negativity. Take a few minutes and list rewarding experiences you have had. Make one list for career-related experiences and another for personal experiences. Examples: Professional – receiving an excellent performance evaluation, successfully organizing a meeting or conference, etc. Personal – graduating from college, successfully skiing an expert slope for the first time, etc.

Professional	Personal

2. What obstacles are keeping you from living a full life? How can you turn those obstacles into challenges? On the left, identify five existing obstacles in your life. Then, on the right, turn those obstacles into challenges.

Obstacles	Challenges

3. What are your self-defeating thoughts? List some of the recurring self-defeating thoughts that limit you personally and professionally.

Professional	Personal

4. Rewrite any self-defeating thoughts so they are less negative. Remember, an obstacle is not really an obstacle, but an opportunity, challenge or learning experience.

_____

_____

_____

_____

5. Write your cue word and possible situations where your cue word will enable you to assume a Posture of Excellence.

_____

_____

_____

_____

_____

_____

Chapter 2
Patterns for Power

SELF-ASSESSMENT

Before reading this chapter, rate yourself on the questions listed below.

How well do you communicate with others?

Not well _____Very well

Have well do you adapt to people you view as different?

Not well_____Very well

How well do you "read people" in their style of working?

Not well_____Very well

Can you effectively get people to do what you want them to do?

Never_____All the time

Does your corporate culture fit or support your personal values?

Not at all _____Perfect fit

Patterns for Power

Most people are hired for their background, technical expertise, and experience. They are fired, transferred or demoted due to the inability to work well with others.

Jan Northup

The Power and Perception of Politics

Employees frequently complain of office politics. They complain of not knowing how to "play the game" or not knowing who the players are or they say that they refuse to play the game. Politics within an organization is often associated with power and with a negative slant. Almost invariably, whether they know it or not, people have failed at the game because they didn't know the players. I don't mean know them by name or position, but rather, know how they communicate, how they make decisions, what motivates them, their work preferences, their strengths and their weaknesses. That's where perception comes in. Individually, politics and power are neither positive nor negative. They only become one or the other as we interact with others and perceive the impact on our work, work satisfaction and personal life.

Successful people know how to identify (perceive) and surround themselves with people who are strong in areas where they have limitations. They know how to elicit those strengths from others for mutual benefit. Too often, people surround themselves with others just like them. While this may feel comfortable, it may lead to organizational and personal blind spots. Your success is not only dependent upon recognizing your own style of interacting, but on your ability to recognize and adapt to the styles of others. This allows you to direct and move others to predetermined outcomes through effective communication and to successful results.

This ability is a powerful tool, and those who have it have the **POWER**! Power? The mere word conjures up Machiavellian images of success-at-all-costs; individuals who would sell their family members to take another step up on the corporate ladder or betray co-workers to get what they want. Power, or wanting power, is not necessarily negative. It doesn't mean having power over some one else in the traditional sense. We are not advocating that you run out and buy a pair of boxing gloves to get a new found sense of power.

It does mean having a power within you that can orchestrate situations and events and move them toward desirable outcomes, ones that you have predetermined. Most would agree that often we go through the motions of getting things done "unconsciously" or "by the seat of our pants." So why not "consciously" determine what we want as successful outcomes and develop the skill(s) that will bring that success? In an eighteen-month research survey, I found that, almost without exception, the respondents reported the ability to communicate with people at all levels within their organization as critical to their success. They also reported that the more adept they became at tapping into highly honed communication skills, the more they experienced positive results, the more powerful they saw themselves and the more others considered them successful.

Let's start by reviewing the steps for developing or improving communication effectiveness:

1. **Understand your personal behavior style preferences.**

    The players in the game of business (and our personal life) generally fall into four distinct behavioral styles: the *Dominant*, the *Influencer*, the *Steady* and the *Compliant*. No one is a pure style. People are a combination of all four styles, but one style is usually more comfortable and becomes their primary style. As you read the general overview of each style, determine which you believe to be your primary style.

    The *Dominant* (D) is the hard-charger, probing, pushing, and often displaying a sense of urgency. A Dominant wants a quick response and the bottom line. If you want the attention of a Dominant, you had better display a high energy level, regardless of the time of day or night. If you go to them with a problem, be prepared to offer solutions. They want to know that you have put thought into resolution and are not just complaining.

The *Influencer* (I) is expressive and engaging. An Influencer is not only a quick thinker, but also an agile talker, cajoling, exhorting, and inducing – but rarely in a coercing manner. The key to succeeding with an Influencer is to take the time to be attentive, to understand their effusive personality and give them time to share their ideas. The Influencer requires your complete loyalty, and expects you to be often and openly impressed with their ability to think creatively and with multiple approaches to any problem resolution.

The *Steady* (S) is laid back, sincere, patient, stable and hard-working. They clear the path, making sure that others have the tools necessary to get the job done. The Steady can be loyal to a fault and caring toward others. They strive to meet the professional, and often personal, needs of their peers and senior colleagues even at the expense of getting their own work done. To succeed with the Steady, follow his or her lead, return loyalty, and show some real initiative by being open about your needs.

The *Compliant* (C) is a stickler for details, covering the bases, crossing every "t" and dotting every "i". A Compliant is methodical, courteous, restrained and holds high standards for self and others. A Compliant does not understand – and will not promote – those who fail to do the same. If you want to impress the Compliant, stick to the facts and figures. Don't "waste" your time or theirs on pipe dreams and visionary schemes.

Which style describes you best? Are you a combination of several? Do you use different styles in different situations?

Clearly, no one is locked into any one of these categories all the time. No one is a pure style, but a combination of factors from all four styles. We use different traits within these styles in different situations; but in each of us, one style is the most comfortable for us (our preferred style) whether thinking about our own communications and interactions or when thinking of someone else's. Your preferred style is the controlling factor in determining what you choose to do and how you produce the results you want. The behavioral traits that make up your style drive:

- How you prefer to solve problems and make decisions
- How you prefer to interact with or influence others
- How you prefer to handle the pace of your environment
- How you prefer to respond to rules, regulations and procedures set by others

A skilled communicator learns how to perceive each style, when to push and when to pull back, when to speak out and when to listen. The knowledge of these preferences is a key criterion for job success, promotion and self-reliance.

2. **Recognize, understand and appreciate others' style preferences.**

After you have a clearer understanding of your own communication and interaction preferences, it is much easier to recognize, understand and appreciate the style preferences of others. There are no right or wrong styles, just different preferences. What type of music do you listen to on the radio? Do all of your friends, family members and co-workers listen to the same type of music? Do some listen to jazz while others listen to country, classical, oldies rock, rap or hip-hop? Who is right? Do you listen to more than one type of music? It may be that your mood or interest at the moment drives which station you listen to.

If I Don't Like Country Music, Will I Go To Hell?

When my son was 7 years old, he came home with a desperate question, "Mom is it true if you don't like county music, you will go to hell when you die?" At first I laughed and then, seeing that he was quite serious, asked, "Why would you think that?" He replied, "Corey's dad told me if I didn't like country music, I would go to hell when I died." Clearly his playmate's dad was joking, but for a 7-year-old this was a serious matter. I told him, "Yes, that's true." Of course, I immediately laughed and told him there was no music that was better or worse. I continued by telling him that liking different music was the same as liking different foods and that it doesn't mean one person is right or wrong.

I have used this example in my communication and team-building workshops since that day. It is a great example of how we each have our preferences, but it doesn't mean the whole world appreciates or enjoys the same way of communicating and performing work tasks. In the same vein, we are all motivated by different rewards or end results of our efforts.

Mom Makes a Lasting Impression

My mother taught me many important lessons, but one of the greatest lessons she ever taught me was about how to view others who were different or had special needs. She had a brother, Harold, born with what was then called infantile paralysis. He was bedridden from birth until his death at the age of 30. He couldn't speak, couldn't feed himself and was totally dependent on others caring for him. My mother said the only response he could give was an occasional smile when she talked to him.

She has often related to me how other kids were so hurtful, making fun of him and calling him names. She never had anger in her voice but rather a tenderness and lovingness as she spoke of my Uncle Harold. I sensed the underlying message: that's just the way it was. He was her brother, an important member of their family and a significant shaper of her values. She always added to the stories about her brother by saying, "He didn't ask to be born that way."

I have heard her use that same saying many times when one of my siblings or I would make "make fun", as children often do, of another child with a disability or who was different from us. It didn't take long until we said less and less hurtful things to or about others (at least in front of our mother). Oh, of course, I was no angel and there were times when I would make fun of someone. If my mother found out, I would get lectured about my actions and would once again hear that he or she didn't ask to be born that way.

I have carried this teaching with me beyond those with physical or mental disabilities to anyone who may be different. It has helped me level out the playing field of differences in the workplace by accepting others' approaches as just the way they like to do things. Less judgment, more tolerance and certainly more opportunities for seeing the world through the eyes of others.

Heightened awareness of the similarities, differences and special needs of each style allows you to use this information as you adapt to others, the third crucial step in the communication process.

3. Adapt for enhanced communication, understanding and relationships.

The savvy employee who understands, identifies and adapts to his or her employer's, direct reports', and co-workers' styles will have the decided advantage. The goal is to develop and participate in win/win situations. This is another form of power. Negative power would result in win/lose situations with short-term benefits. When both parties walk away from a conversation, negotiation or meeting feeling they were heard, understood and involved, the benefits are long-term.

One of the most frequently requested services from my clients are communication workshops. Many of you have probably taken one or more of these seminars as they are still as popular today as they were 26 years ago when I started my company. That always raises the question, why haven't we solved our communications problems, especially with so many communications seminars on the market? Organizations want people who can collaborate, cooperate and communicate well within their teams and across team boundaries. We all know those people who should wear a t-shirt with words of warning, *"Does not play well with others."*

To further understand each style and develop specific

strategies for adapting to others, you can build on the general characteristics already presented by looking at the specific strengths and possible limitations. Strengths highlight areas where you may excel in higher levels of productivity and success.

Possible Strengths

- A (D) is strong in creative problem solving, risk-taking, decision making, establishing and utilizing authority,
  and is task-oriented and a catalyst for change.
- An (I) is strong in working with people, interfacing with the community, helping others, motivating people, articulating ideas, creating positive learning/working environments, making favorable impressions and instilling a lighthearted or humorous feeling in others.
- An (S) is strong in patience, loyalty to people and organizations, concentration, listening, long-term commitments, specializing, calming others and maintaining the status quo.
- A (C) is strong in systematic thinking, following directions and cooperating with standard procedures, showing attention to details, working in restrictive or controlled environments, critical thinking, maintaining status quo and using diplomatic verbal skills.

Just as each style has its strengths, each style has possible limitations that may keep them from achieving peak performance and maximum productivity. For example, because (D)s are good at directing others, they may need to work on compromise. Because (I)s are so verbal, they may need to work on listening skills. Because (S)s don't adapt easily to change, they may need to work on functioning in unpredictable environments. Because (C)s work so well with facts and figures, they may need to be more sensitive to the emotional (personal) side of an issue.

Possible Limitations

- A (D) may need to strengthen or refine skills in researching, evaluating and using facts, being more cautious, risk-taking and decision making based on information and deliberation. A (D) may need to concentrate on development of a more varied voice, utilization of gestures, sensitivity to feelings, acceptance of working with others, stress management, patience and ability to compromise.
- An (I) may need to strengthen or refine skills in logical thinking, utilizing research and facts, concentration, working alone, maintaining objectivity and evaluating new ideas. An (I) may need to curtail socialization on the job, work with technology versus people, be less ideological, set realistic deadlines and improve listening skills and attention to detail.
- An (S) may need to strengthen or refine skills in risk-taking, critical thinking, maintaining objectivity, diversifying tasks, functioning in unpredictable environments and adjusting to change.

- A (C) may need to strengthen or refine skills in public speaking, delegating, decision making, self-esteem, presenting opposing views, offering ideas and concepts as opposed to facts and figures, accepting sudden change, and being flexible and sensitive to others' feelings.

Most people have had communication experiences where they were convinced the other person was speaking another language. The styles described above have often been referred to as "languages." When one person is speaking Dominance and the other person is speaking or listening in Compliance, it may indeed seem like one is speaking a foreign language. This is validated when one set of instructions is given and yet another set carried out. With insight into the characteristics of the four styles, both strengths and possible limitations, instructions and feedback can be adapted for the greatest effectiveness. The sender of information can adapt to the language of the receiver, ensuring that the receiver is hearing the information in his or her "language."

Let me give you a scenario that will help illustrate each style. Although somewhat exaggerated, it humorously points out the strengths and limitations of each style. As you read, keep these questions in mind: Can you identify yourself? Does someone else come to mind?

The Morning Greeting

Complaining that you woke up with a sore throat, here

are some typical responses that you might expect from the four styles:

- The (D) would scold you with, "Well, did you call a doctor?" A (D) is only interested in hearing the solution to the problem.
- The (I) would say, "Oh, you have a sore throat? Me too! And, you know, my stomach doesn't feel very good either." It's not one-upmanship but, rather, their way of saying, "I am with you baby. I feel your pain."
- The (S) will sympathetically call you around their desk, open the bottom drawer displaying a mini-pharmacy, and offer you one of numerous cold-relief remedies from herbal tea, cough drops, aspirins, and of course, chicken soup.
- The (C), with hands on hips, will exclaim, "Well, what do you expect? Did you know thirty-three percent of people your age experience sore throats in the month of February?" All you wanted was a little sympathy and you received the latest statistics from the American Medical Association.

Now you've explored the different styles and reviewed several scenarios, how can you put this information to use? There are three main functions that can be addressed by using what you know about interactive styles:

1. Gain the commitment and cooperation of others.
2. Build effective teams.
3. Resolve and prevent conflict.

Gain the Commitment and Cooperation of Others

First, you can increase your ability to gain the commitment and cooperation from those around you. People tend to trust and work well with those who seem like themselves. The way to gain commitment and cooperation is to adapt to their style. You need to get into their world and understand them before you can blend your styles for the most productive relationships. I've had managers laugh or even fold their arms and exclaim, "Listen, I'm in charge around here. If anyone is going to change their style, it's going to be them, not me!"

I can understand this immediate response. They've paid their dues, they've worked their way into a management position, and they've earned the right to be in charge and expect people to do things their way. And yet, if it is true that a manager could quickly gain the commitment and the cooperation of others, wouldn't it be in her best interest to adapt to their style? Wouldn't it be in your best interest to adapt to the styles of people around you to achieve your goals personally as well as professionally?

Here is a simple example to reinforce this idea that we gravitate toward people who seem most like us. When you walk into a room full of people, such as a meeting or social occasion, who do you look for first? Naturally, you look for someone you already know. If you do not see anyone you know, you begin reading people either consciously or unconsciously, to see if they would be someone with whom you would be comfortable. You do not walk in and look for the strangest person in the room to sit by. You move toward someone who is dressed similarly, is the same gender, the same height, the same race, or whose posture and body language are open and friendly. We are more comfortable around those who seem like ourselves.

The following observations should provide additional clues about another person's style, but be careful jumping to conclusions. It takes time for people to drop their masks and become comfortable with new acquaintances. Listen carefully and observe.

The next time you enter someone's office, look around the room. Does it have a feeling of power or warmth? How is it decorated? Family pictures? Plaques and trophies? Charts and graphs? Diplomas? Scenic artwork? What kinds of books do you see? How is the furniture arranged? Are the chairs arranged so you sit next to the person or across from them?

Listen to the words spoken. Does the person tend to speak in terms of "I, me, mine and yours" or "ours, us and we?" Does the conversation center more on tasks or people? Does the person strike you as being more emotional or more logical?

Listen to what isn't being said. Does the person listen more than talk? Do they use hand gestures? Is their speech animated? What does their body language say to you? Do they ask a lot of questions or give simple and direct answers?

All of these are important clues to the styles of others. Understanding their pattern of interaction gives you the edge in gaining commitment and cooperation. That knowledge is power. It puts you in control.

Build Effective Teams

Second, you can build more effective teams by being aware of styles. Opposite styles can be more effective in a team because they pay attention to different aspects of a problem. Two task-oriented styles may spend their time arguing about philosophical and procedural differences, while two people-oriented styles may spend too much time over coffee planning what they are going to do rather than just doing it. Two like styles may be comfortable initially, but less productive in the long run. When building a team, you may need all styles. There is no way to generalize without knowing the specific tasks involved. You must first determine the kind of tasks or end results that you want. You may actually need only one style if all of the tasks require the same skills and characteristics.

A marketing department may need a (D) to develop a long-range strategy, an (I) to design the logo and motto and create a media campaign, an (S) to input and coordinate activities and schedules and a (C) to gather market data related to demographics, customer base, pricing structure and profit-loss projections.

Another organization may only provide research data to another department or customer. In that case, they may only need individuals who are strong in gathering specific information and details and preparing reports or presentations that are thorough and accurate in the data. This may require (S) or (C) styles. As a manager or supervisor this information can be the driving factor in developing, organizing and maintaining high-achieving teams.

Resolve and Prevent Conflict

Third, you can employ conflict resolution or conflict prevention strategies. Let me give you the example of Pat and her supervisor Rhonda.

Pat liked working for Rhonda and Rhonda respected Pat's subject matter expertise, but they would get totally frustrated working together. So, after eight years of working together, they attended one of my workshops and completed a style assessment. They discovered they were opposite styles. Rhonda was a (D) – only interested in the bottom line and the big picture. Pat was a (C) – the detail person; very data- and research-oriented. She wanted specific directions and ample guidance when she was given an assignment. Rhonda, on the other hand, would assign a project to Pat, giving only the outcome desired with no how-to details. Feeling frustrated with the lack of direction, Pat would return with questions or concerns. Rhonda would become frustrated with Pat for wasting time with questions when she should be working.

Pat wanted detailed instructions in the beginning to be sure she was going in the right direction so she wouldn't have to start over. When Pat would complete a project and present the findings, she would literally read page after page of facts and figures to Rhonda before getting to the point. Rhonda only wanted the bottom line or to hear the summary paragraph; she wasn't concerned with all the facts and figures Pat used to come up with the answer. On the other hand, it's important to remember that Rhonda's style wants to know there is data available to substantiate the information she is given.

Once they understood each other's style, they were able to adapt to each other's needs and begin a new, productive relationship. Now they even joke about their differences. If Rhonda gives Pat a project without enough instruction, Pat simply says, "Now you know my style needs more detail." If Rhonda finds Pat giving her too much data she says, "Now remember, Pat, (D)s only need the bottom line."

With insight into the characteristics of the four styles, your own and others, you will increase your power. You will be able to work with people of all styles and at all levels. Adapting to those differences will allow you to direct and lead others to the outcomes you desire. Using the D.I.S.C. model as one tool, you can gain a better understanding of your preferred way of working and relating to others, as well as allowing you to recognize the styles of others. Understanding your personal style will give you greater control over your life.

In conclusion, if the most important skill for advancement is communicating and interacting effectively with others, wouldn't you want to refine this skill? Of course you would. By now you should have identified your primary style, your preferred way of communicating and interacting with others. You also should have been able to identify the primary style of those with whom you interact on a regular basis, both in your work environment and your home environment. In Chapter 3, Positioning, strategies for motivating each style and recommendations for presenting to each style will be explored.

The following can serve as a quick reference as you continue to evaluate your own strengths and the strengths of others and develop strategies for adapting your style for maximum communication effectiveness.

STYLE MATRIX I
Possible Strengths

Dominant	Influencer
Creative problem solving	Working with people
Risk-taking	Motivating people
Achieving desired outcomes	Articulating ideas
Being precise in use of time	Creating positive working environments
Establishing and using authority	Interfacing with the community
Steady	**Compliant**
Listening carefully	Following directions
Maintaining status quo	Showing attention to detail
Specializing	Cooperating with procedures
Calming others	Using time efficiently and effectively
Giving long-term commitments	Conducting research

STYLE MATRIX II
Possible Limitations

Dominant	Influencer
Researching and using facts	Utilizing research and facts
Sensitivity to feelings	Staying focused on one task
Listening to all facts before deciding	Working alone
Day-to-day planning	Listening skills
Compromising	Setting realistic deadlines
Steady	**Compliant**
Risk-taking	Delegating
Diversifying tasks	Accepting sudden change
Functioning in unpredictable environments	Sensitivity to feelings
Adjusting to change	Public speaking skills
Objectivity	Quick decision making

Reinforcement Activities

1. In reviewing your preferences, list your strengths related to each style. The more strengths you have listed under a particular style may point to the style that is your preference or the one that is more comfortable for you.

Dominant	Influencer
Steady	**Compliant**

2. To avoid embarrassing misunderstandings and to improve communications, we need to be aware of the styles of others. Using the following questions as a guide, determine the style of three people with whom you personally interact on a regular basis.

    A. How do they get people to do what they want them to do?

    B. What are some of their pet peeves about people?

    C. What are some of their favorite things to do?

    D. Describe their home.

Person # 1 Name _____

Observations_____

Style _____

Person #2 Name _____

Observations_____

Style _____

Person #3 Name _____

Observations_____

Style _____

3. The same activity can help you identify the styles of people at work. This will enable you to quickly gain their commitment and cooperation. Think of three co-workers with whom you interact on a regular basis. Answer the questions listed below and write down what you believe to be their primary style.

   A. How do they get people to do what they want them to do?

   B. What are some of their pet peeves about the people with whom they work?

   C. What are some of their favorite tasks/jobs?

   D. Describe their office environment or office furnishings.

Person # 1 Name_____

Observations_____

Style _____

Person #2 Name _____

Observations _____

Style _____

Person #3 Name _____

Observations _____

Style _____

4. List some of the immediate positive changes that could occur in your communications as a result of having a better understanding of the four key styles.

_____

_____

_____

_____

_____

_____

_____

_____

_____

_____

Chapter 3
Positioning

SELF-ASSESSMENT

Before reading this chapter, rate yourself on the questions listed below.

To what extent is your energy level influenced by others?
Not at all_____Very much

How well do you know and understand your own strengths and capabilities?
Not at all _____Very well

How helpful do you feel a mentor/coach would be to your career?
Not at all _____Essential

How often do you trust your intuition?
Never_____All the time

How would you rate your ability to speak before a group?
Scared to death _____Fantastic

How would you rate your writing skills?
None _____Exceptional

How well do you feel you currently "fit in" with your organization?
Not at all _____Very well

Positioning

It's not our talents that define us, but our choices.

J.K. Rowling, from
Harry Potter

Sorry, Positioning is NOT the sex education portion of the book! Positioning, in this chapter, is surrounding yourself with an environment for professional success. Today, when we talk of Positioning, we are really talking about three types of Positioning. The first type is maintaining a personal support system; the second, taking advantage of a professional support system; and third, developing skills that allow you to take advantage of opportunities as they arise. It's positioning yourself with other people and new skills that will multiply your efforts. Strategically, it means "the whole is greater than the sum of its parts."

Personal Support System

Women we surveyed reported that, other than personal characteristics developed early in life, the most important factor for success in creating balance in their personal and professional lives was having the wholehearted support of a spouse, a family member or another significant person in their life. This person was their sounding board; the person who believed in them, their dreams, and their goals, and the person who would stand by them or even push them in a positive way to reach their goals.

In addition to your immediate family, your personal support system includes your friends. They are part of your emotional network – the network you need, because shared joy is double joy and shared sorrow is half sorrow. Friends expand your safe environment. Chosen wisely, they are nonjudgmental. *A friend is someone who can see through you and still enjoy the show.* Often neglected in the hustle and bustle of your life, when you need to turn to them, your friends are still there. A personal support system might also include a mental health professional such as a counselor or therapist who can offer you specific strategies for dealing with the competing demands of a career and personal life. Although she is a professional, she can be a valuable part of the personal support system. She is trained to provide a safe, objective environment while you work through problems you can't solve alone. You may need her more at certain points in your life, especially during critical incidents. Most turn to her in desperation to help put back the pieces after falling apart when instead she should be used to help keep the pieces intact along the way.

Pause for a moment. Who are the people who nurture and console you? Are you surrounded by Energy Givers or Energy Robbers? Everyone knows what an Energy Giver is. It's the person who pumps you up when you are down. It's the person who gets excited for you when you share with them even your smallest accomplishment. It's the person who gives you a pat on the back for encouragement or a kick in the pants when you are ready to give up. Energy Givers are the people who greet you in the hallway with a smile and are always ready with a "Good morning, how are you?"

You also know who Energy Robbers are. They're the people who greet you in the hall with a grumble and when you say "Good morning," they say, "What's good about it?" When you say, "Isn't it a beautiful day," they say, "It's supposed to rain this afternoon." When you share with them that your supervisor just told you the report you turned in was one of the best she had ever read, they say, "She told me the same thing last week."

Meat Grinders, Chew Them Up and Spit Them Out

You need to be even more aware of the meat grinders. They not only rob your energy, but aggressively go after you hoping to grind you up and spit you out destroying your enthusiasm and Prosperity Thinking. They are rarely subtle, but rather, openly criticize with words, gestures, looks, and even rumors that they know are untrue or other "back biting" techniques. Their purpose is to make you look bad so they look better. Somewhere along the road of life, they lost their positive self-esteem.

While it is true that no one can literally give or rob you of your energy, there are people who seem to create an environment where you feel energized or drained.

There is no question that when you interact with others you are impacted in ways that affect your mental, physical and emotional energy. When you interact with an Energy Robber you are sucked into a kind of negativity that pulls you down, short-circuits your energy, and puts the fire out that are your hopes, positive thoughts and purposeful actions. Luckily, you have Energy Givers in your life. When you interact with them, you have a sense of satisfaction, happiness and increased motivations, and life is good! Events, whether recurring occasionally or often, can also be Energy Givers or Energy Robbers. Take a moment to list the Energy Givers and Energy Robbers in your life.

Energy Givers	Energy Robbers
Events	Events
Relationships	Relationships

Did you find yourself trying to decide which list to put someone on, or did you find you wanted to put the same person or event on both lists? When you spend a lot of time with someone or have repeated experiences with them, it creates the opportunity to experience them as both an Energy Giver and an Energy Robber. I have to admit that I've put some of the most significant people in my life on both lists.

It is also a good idea to ask yourself how you are an Energy Giver or an Energy Robber. This awareness can often help in correcting communication or interaction problems with the people around you. There may be times when you are being an Energy Giver to someone else, you expend so much of your own energy that it turns into an Energy Robbing situation. Conversely, being an Energy Giver to someone else can give you an energy boost. There may be times when your own stress causes you to be Energy Robber. You can probably think of times when stress at work has caused you to go home and kick your dog, and you don't even have a dog!

Surrounding yourself with Energy Givers and avoiding the negative impact of Energy Robbers is a skill. When this skill is employed, it can improve the quality of your personal and professional lives. Find ways to increase time spent with the Energy Givers in your life. Although you can't always avoid Energy Robbers, either personally or professionally, you can counteract any negative impact by employing the Posture of Excellence. Don't let them rain on your parade. You are the Grand Marshall of your parade through life and those around you will either be in the marching band or they just might get run over if they step in front of you with their negativity!

You can't live with them and you can't leave them beside the road.

If the Cape Fits, Wear It!

If not, throw it out or put it on e-Bay and let some other woman try it on for size. Taking good care of your career takes an incredible amount of energy. Taking good care of yourself and your family takes an incredible amount of energy. Ok, so how do you do it all? Most women can relate to the *superwoman syndrome*, trying to be all things to all people. The result is that our cape is tattered from flying from one responsibility to another.

Even though this was more than 25 years ago, I can vividly remember working, going to graduate school two nights a week, co-managing a business, preparing meals, keeping my house clean just in case it had to undergo the "white gloves" test and the list goes on and on. Oh, did I mention that was even before my son was born? I was determined to get my Ph.D as a way to better myself, increase my earning power, and to be able to provide more for my family. Great motivations, right? What I found were others looking over the top of their glasses at me. You know "the look." Of course there were the questions accompanied by that certain smile that would take the air out of my balloon of hopes and dreams. So, when was I going to start a family? Or, more accurately, when were my mother and mother-in-law going to get a grandbaby? Why did I miss the picnic? In other words, your poor husband had to go by himself because you were too busy studying for finals. With that same smile (by now I saw it more as an evil sneer) women would tell me I couldn't do it all and would have to make a choice. I could either work or I could have a family. How dare they question my abilities! Then there was the proverbial battle with my own ego and stubbornness. I could do it all! Just watch me. The naysayers would see.

Before long, I was burning the candle at both ends trying to do it all and, quite frankly, I was exhausted. The long hours were a part of the exhaustion, but I think what drained me most was battling the social stigma that I had to choose between a career and a family. I was haunted by the image of being a successful, but lonely, career woman while at the same time seeing myself with a house full of children; hair tied back wearing an old shirt with Gerber's strained peas down the front and with a laundry basket in one arm and a screaming child in the other.

My first true understanding of the importance of a personal support system was when my husband offered to have someone help us clean the house. He too was working, going to school, and co-managing our business. He believed in my dream of going on for more education and could not have cared less if I missed the damn picnic. I also had a good friend who told me, when I tried to bring her into my pity party, that she believed that women could do it all, just not at the same time, and there were trade-offs. At about the same time a close male friend said he admired me for everything I was trying to do and then followed with advice that had taken him from a workaholic to peace with himself. "You have to stop and smell the roses. You are so driven you may miss some incredible opportunity right in front of you. Slow down and look around for the unexpected."

From that point on, I had to decide if it was more important to dust the furniture, study, or go to a social function. More importantly, I took time to reevaluate my goals from time to time just in case that opportunity was calling me and I was too busy to answer it. As they say, the rest is history, my history, and I am thankful I learned that my cape may not always be clean and pressed but with a personal support system of a significant other, my family and my friends, I can still fly toward what I want in life.

There Was An Old Woman Who Lived In A Shoe!

She certainly didn't know what to do, and neither do most of the rest of us when you add children into the equation of balancing career and home. My superwoman saga continued as I added the blessed event in my life, the birth of my son. By now I had my own business and was traveling two to three weeks a month speaking nationally and abroad. Now what do I do with a child? I was allowed two carry-ons and that is just what I did. I loved being with my son so I took him with me when I could. Of course, there were times he couldn't travel with me. Enter child care. If you are a working mother, you may have faced the dilemma of finding the right person or child care center that would give your child what he or she needed when you weren't there.

If you have good child care, you can give your attention to your job; if not, you will be distracted and unable to give your attention to your job. I tried all of the options from live-in help to dragging my son and all of his worldly belongings off to a private home to dropping him off at a child care center. They all had their pluses and minuses but I don't think I ever felt confident that he was getting the love and attention that I could have given him! Then some early and now more recent research suggested that child care was probably the best thing for him, despite my "mother hen" attitude.

While studies vary on specific developmental issues when children are in the care of others, most long-term studies have found that children of working mothers score higher on IQ tests, have better communication and conflict resolution skills, are independent thinkers, and could problem solve better than those who stayed home with mothers who didn't work.

According to the U.S. Department of Labor, an estimated 71 percent of mothers of children eighteen and younger are in the labor force compared to my first research in 1985 when only 62 percent were. The following chart demonstrates that working mothers are major contributors to the workforce and may need to deal with child care issues in order to allow them the flexibility and freedom to meet the demands of their career. It is also interesting to note that the percentage dropped from 2000 to 2004.

| Percentage of mothers with children | | | |
Year	Under 18 years	6 to 17 years	Under 6 years
1985	62.1	69.9	53.5
1990	66.7	74.7	58.2
1995	69.7	76.4	62.3
2000	72.9	79.0	65.3
2004	70.7	77.5	62.2

Working mothers are and will continue to be in the work force. If you are a working mother, you will have to choose child care options that fit with your values and your professional goals. Making trade-offs or delaying certain career choices in favor of your children's needs is your decision and your decision alone. When you are making choices based on your present and potential future, then you will make the right choices, and the opinions, comments or "smiles" of others will not distract you from those choices.

From Diapers to Depends

In the spirit of discussing your care-giving responsibilities, you may find yourself faced with a new responsibility: caring for an elderly friend or family member. As a Baby Boomer, conversations with others my age have gravitated away from talking about our children to the current and future needs of our aging parents. Thrown in of course are our concerns about our own needs as we continue aging.

While many aging adults are in great health, others need the same kind of support, attention and care-giving as children. Having the time and energy required for finding the appropriate elder care resources, making medical, financial or legal decisions, or providing transportation when their mobility has been compromised may have thrown you back into the balancing act between work and home. Your cape is long gone but your need to return to being superwoman may loom. This is another critical time in your life when a personal support system is crucial to your success.

Professional Support System

The second type of Positioning – a professional support system – includes mentors, coaches, advisors, peers or anyone else who can help you as you grow within your job or your profession. It is a well-established fact of economic life that your efforts will be enhanced by favorable alliances. You can put the same principle to work for your career by surrounding yourself with people and skills that multiply your efforts.

First, find a mentor. A mentor is someone who offers you the wisdom of their experience. They can challenge you to look at your goals or they can propel you into action. During my research women told me they more quickly reached success when they had a professional mentor or coach. The terms mentor and coach are often used interchangeably, which is okay. The important part is that a mentor can assess your skill gaps and then can be or can direct you to those who serve as a:

- **Teacher** – Providing theoretical or technical learning opportunities.
- **Guide** – Sharing organizational insight.
- **Counselor** – Asking, listening and supporting.
- **Challenger** – Uncovering blind spots.
- **Role Model** – Demonstrating through actions.
- **Door Opener** – Facilitating new contacts and your visibility.

I've often been asked, "What if there isn't a woman in my organization who could mentor me?" Ideally, choosing a woman for a mentor (or choosing a woman to mentor) is supporting the belief that women should be helping other women. But I also know that, realistically, there may not be a woman in your organization who has advanced to the position to which you aspire, or who has the experience necessary to mentor you. So choose the person, male or female, who can best support your efforts and who can contribute to your professional growth.

It is interesting to note, in almost every case, the men we interviewed reported they were assigned a mentor when they began a new job or as they progressed in the organization. Whether formally or informally, they were taught about the financial operations, the politics, the unspoken rules for getting ahead, and the dues they would have to pay to be seen as a team player. Women, on the other hand, reported that they were rarely assigned a mentor. Instead, someone would teach them a specific job, but when it came to learning the organizational issues and opportunities, they had to seek out mentors on their own.

Choosing a mentor is very important. Your mentor should be the most knowledgeable and experienced person in the organization. Women often ask me if there isn't a danger of gossip if you have a male mentor. The answer is, yes! Of course, whenever a man and woman work together, there is the chance that co-workers and friends may question your professional relationship. If that happens, tell them to mind their own business! Oh, I guess that is not politically correct; so here's another option. Be open and honest about the support and mentoring the other person is providing. Just by addressing the issue head on, you will counteract most potential problems. Notice I said most. There are going to be those who are busybodies or those who like to stir up the dirt on anyone in close range. Don't worry about them; just do what you need to do to reach your goals.

Whether your current boss or supervisor can serve as a mentor depends on the person. Some supervisors actively mentor and view the success of their employees as a demonstration of their own abilities. Others fear losing good employees and only focus on the challenges of training someone to fill the vacant position. Still others see employees as a threat and fear for their own job if they teach them everything they know.

Mentors change as you grow professionally. Reassess your career goals every few months and determine if your current mentor is contributing to those goals. You may also have several mentors at the same time for different aspects of your career. The only caution is to know that you may receive conflicting advice or assistance if you have too many mentors.

Oh, Mentor, Where Art Thou?

How do you find a mentor? If you identify someone you think would make a great mentor, ask her! What's the worst she can say? More than likely she will be flattered that you asked her. She then may move into wondering what she has to do, how much time it will take, and whether she can really help you. Take time to discuss your reason for asking her (a little ego stroking is good here) and talk about the logistics of when and where you could meet and how much time she could give. Since you are asking a favor, let her take the lead on the location and time that is most convenient for her.

Why would anyone want to spend time with you? After all there is not usually any form of payment unless you are working with a professional coach. In assisting numerous organizations develop and implement formalized mentoring programs, I have heard the following over and over and over …

- Someone helped me and now I can give back.
- I have had to keep on my toes to answer technical questions.
- It has helped me spot the talents in my own people.

- It's good for the whole organization when a person increases their skills.
- Hey, when they do great things, I look good. (Think that is a (D) talking?).
- With turnover rates, I can build potential replacements.

Me, a Mentor?

Mentoring others and encouraging them to become what they want helps you build a loyal support system. When you empower others, you empower yourself, and when you help one woman grow professionally, you help all women.

As a part of your professional network, you will also need advisors. An advisor is a paid professional, such as a lawyer, banker, accountant or financial planner, who supports your efforts. Since you're paying a professional for advice, take that advice! Go first class with your advisors! Let each one do what she does best.

Just as one would go to a dentist for a toothache, not an obstetrician, use specialists. For legal advice, go to a lawyer, for advice on banking go to a banker, for advice on taxes go to an accountant, and for money management advice go to a financial planner. You will need all of them as your success grows. Make sure you are comfortable with their interactive style. My attorney has a similar style as I do. She knows how to cut through the details and give me a bottom line recommendation. At times it is better to use an advisor with a different style from your own. My accountant is a (C). She keeps me on track by pressing for deadlines and details that aren't my strong points.

And, finally, among your professional support system you will need your professional colleagues. Networking with other professionals and belonging to professional organizations can help you keep abreast of current trends and challenges in your career field. It can provide a forum to discuss personal issues related to your career and can allow you to meet people who could become a part of your personal and professional support system.

So far we've discussed Positioning in terms of individuals, mentors, advisors and professional colleagues, but you must also consider the organization for which you work. There is much written today about corporate cultures and corporate styles. A corporate style is "the way we do things around here." It reflects the principles upon which the organization is built. This philosophical foundation determines how the company directs business, how it manages employees, and the informal rules and feelings about everyday behavior. Be aware that an organization will have its own style and you may need to position yourself within that organization to fit that style. Better still, choose an organization that fits your style.

A company's style can be identified by its values and the climate it creates. There are clues to watch for. Ask yourself if the company you work for, or in which you are interested, is conservative or avant-garde, cluttered or organized, informal or rigid, warm or cool? For example, if you're a freewheeling (I), and work in a company with a meticulous (C) style, be aware that you will need to adapt. Often, when your style doesn't match the corporate style, your tendency is to blame yourself or to blame the company for any difficulties. Have you ever had difficulty fitting into an organization? Consider that the difficulty may have been an incompatibility of styles, not a deficiency of either party. How do you fit into your company today? Does it fit your style? Make sure you're comfortable with your company's style and that your company is supportive of your style.

We've talked about how you can position yourself with personal and professional support systems. Now you're going to explore the third type of Positioning:

Positioning Yourself With Specific Skills

Positioning yourself with specific skills that will allow you to take advantage of opportunities as they arise. There are four skills that we've found to be the most essential:

1. Working effectively with others.
2. Writing well.
3. Speaking before a group.
4. Trusting your intuition.

Working Effectively With Others

The first skill, as we learned in Patterns for Power, is being able to quickly assess the styles of others and to effectively work with them. This skill can be learned and practiced, especially when briefing and motivating others.

The motivation of others to provide you with the results you want is directly related to how you present ideas and information to them. For maximum briefing effectiveness, the following guidelines are suggested. These guidelines may be used when presenting information in formal classroom training, in one-on-one instruction, or when giving a speech or briefing an individual or a group.

To Present Information to an Dominant

- Be precise and to the point
- Offer innovative ideas
- Don't bother with the details
- Get to the bottom line
- Get to the problem and leave the Dominant in control

To Present Information to an Influencer

- Provide a warm and friendly environment
- Allow them the opportunity to talk
- Include feelings and opinions in your presentation
- Leave the details for later

To Present Information to a Steady

- Brief them in a sincere, personal manner
- Draw them out and ask questions to get their opinion
- Present new ideas in a low-key manner
- Assure them of their importance to the team

To Present Information to a Compliant

- Present ideas step-by-step
- Clearly state objectives
- Give the pros and cons of the plan
- Back up plan with solid and organized data

No matter where you work, whether it's for a corporation, a government agency or yourself, you're always motivating others for maximum cooperation. To help maintain their high performance, the following guidelines are suggested.

To Motivate a Dominant

- Give them authority
- Challenge them with difficult assignments
- Give them freedom
- Reward them with advancement and prestige

To Motivate an Influencer

- Offer them variety
- Give them opportunity to share with others
- Press them for deadlines
- Reward them with recognition

To Motivate a Steady

- Offer them job security
- Give them their own work space and time for adjustment
- Demonstrate conventional policies and procedures
- Provide encouragement and support from management

To Motivate a Compliant

- Motivate them with logic
- Give them jobs that require precision
- Show them they are important as a person and not just because of the job they do
- Recognize their high standards of excellence

Being able to relate to specific styles when briefing and motivating people ensures commitment and cooperation from those around you. People work with you rather than against you.

Writing Well

The second skill is the ability to write well. If you write well, people quickly conclude that you are intelligent. If you are intelligent but don't write well it takes you far longer to convince others of your abilities. If a majority of your correspondences are through e-mail, you can determine how to send the correct message along with the words that are read. Depending on the nature of the e-mail, you can also determine when you may need to spend more time composing and presenting information in a more formalized and logical way. You can also determine when abbreviated messages are appropriate and, even then, you need to write them in such a way that the intent of your message is communicated. It may be helpful for you to take a professional or technical writing course. These are often given on-site by organizations. Check with your training department.

Speaking Before a Group

The third skill is the ability to speak before a group, which builds confidence and credibility, and gives you visibility. Hopefully, you will speak on those topics that you know best, as this reduces some of the stress many people experience when speaking. Most people are comfortable in speaking to their colleagues individually, but begin to lose their self-confidence when asked to speak to a group. People tend to grant authority to those who can speak confidently on a subject. Public speaking still holds first place on the list of adults' fears, ranking above fear of high places, snakes and even death. There are many courses on public speaking, as well as several organizations that meet for the specific purpose of providing practice in public speaking.

You can probably think of examples where a person who was an expert on her subject stepped to the front of the room and did not present well. Another person stepped to the front of the room and you knew that she was not as well versed, but she was fluent and convincing in her speaking. Was she perceived as knowing more? That is usually the case and just another reason that women should hone their speaking skills as a way of demonstrating their knowledge and competence.

Trusting Your Intuition

The fourth skill is trusting your intuition. While it is true that we weigh the pros and cons of making a decision or deciding on a course of action, the final decision often comes down to trusting that internal awareness that one aspect over the other "feels right." I have had many people share stories with me where they had a long list of rational reasons why they should or shouldn't have made a certain decision. They felt that something just wasn't right or the odds seemed to be stacked against them, but they went with the direction that felt right and it ended up being the right decision. Can you think of a time when you trusted your intuition? What was the outcome?

Intuition is a fascinating gift that we all have and one that you can use to your advantage. Men don't call it intuition. They call it a gut-level reaction, or shooting from the hip. Acting on intuition has traditionally been a woman's strong point. Trust your intuitive sense and use it as an everyday skill as you face decisions in your life.

These four skills – working effectively with others, writing well, speaking before groups, and trusting your intuition – will put you in a position to take advantage of opportunities as they occur.

In summary, remember the three types of Positioning that should be integrated into your life. The first is your personal support system, the second is your professional support system, and the third is developing skills that allow you to take advantage of opportunities as they arise.

Out With the Energy Robbers!

We have all experienced relationships that have affected our personal and professional lives, good relationships as well as those that have not been supportive. To make you strong for any negative relationship in the future, recall a past relationship or situation that still haunts you as being a sour or bitter experience. Because there is a tendency to remember that experience negatively with a hangover of bitter feelings, you will want to negate those bad feelings by releasing them. Release any resentment or grievance you hold toward another. Holding grudges toward people and events is an energy robber.

The late Elizabeth Kubler-Ross, M.D., told me, "Time doesn't heal; it only festers if there is no resolution." It may be necessary to acknowledge and express any anger that you may feel. I want to give you the opportunity to resolve any suppressed anger or negativity. You can replace your negative self-talk with more positive self-talk and make those thoughts your dominant thoughts. You will once again use the Posture of Excellence activity as you recall any negative self-talk that you want to replace.

Practice Application

Read the instructions completely so that you understand the practice application process. After you have done that, try it out!

- Get into a comfortable position with music playing softly in the background.
- Close your eyes.
- Take several deep breaths as you relax with the music.
- Focus on a past negative job, relationship or event that is keeping you from focusing positively on your

unlimited potential. Acknowledge and accept that those feelings and thoughts do exist.

- Repeat your cue word as you begin to release those negative thoughts or feelings. Now release those thoughts and feelings. Release them generously and lovingly because, in so doing, you feel generous and abundant and better about yourself. Feeling good about yourself is an Energy Giver.

- Now recall an especially joyful time during a relationship that went bad, or recall something good that came out of a job that soured. Focus on something good that you learned from that relationship, interaction or job.

- As the music continues, reflect on that.

- Silently give thanks for all opportunities that have helped you grow and evolve personally and professionally. The ending of a relationship or a job that soured, as painful as it may have been, perhaps freed you to being open to an experience that you had been closed to before.

- Silently give thanks for that.

- You may have gained insight, a new awareness of how to recognize and avoid people or situations that are not supportive.

- Silently give thanks for that.

- Let any negativity go. Remember living well is the best revenge.

- Silently repeat these or similar affirmations as you

69

release negative memories and position yourself for a positive, successful future.

❖ *I release negative feelings.*

❖ *I am letting go.*

❖ *A Promotable Woman feels generous and abundant.*

❖ *I am feeling generous and abundant.*

❖ *I am a Promotable Woman.*

• Remain relaxed with your eyes closed as you continue to feel good about your successes. Then, whenever you are ready, slowly stretch your arms and legs, feeling energized and wide awake with renewed vitality.

This poem by Peter McWilliams is a beautiful affirmation of our ability to move forward.

Sifting through the
ashes of our relationship

I find many things
to be grateful for.

I can say "thank you" for
warm mornings,
cold protein drinks,
and the love you have offered
another.

I can say "thank you"
for being there
willing to be shared.

I can say "thank you" for
the countless poems you were
the inspiration for and the
many changes you were
catalyst to.

But how, in my grasp of
the English Language,
faltering as it is,
can I ever

thank you
for
Beethoven?

Reinforcement Activities

1. Set a timer for three minutes. List all of your strengths, everything that you are good at personally or professionally. Be sure to include all of your skills, including changing the oil in the car, talking on the phone, giving directions, synthesizing data, organizing scout troops or organizing conferences.

   _____

   _____

   _____

   _____

2. How can these strengths be more fully developed? What can you do every day to maximize and strengthen all of the positive characteristics listed above? How can these personal skills and characteristics transition into helping you increase your professional productivity?

   _____

   _____

   _____

   _____

   _____

3. It is recommended that you surround yourself with professional advisors. List any advisors who are currently within your support structure and add any new advisors you will be seeking:

Banker _____

Accountant _____

Financial Planner _____

Lawyer_____

Mental Health Professional_____

4. WANTED: ONE MENTOR. Examine your career today and then project into your future. What do you need in a mentor right now to help achieve your future career goals?

_____

_____

_____

_____

5. Who could serve as your mentor? _____

_____

6. Who could you mentor? _____

_____

_____

7. How would you describe the company you are currently working with; conservative, avant-garde, cluttered, organized, informal, rigid?

_____

_____

_____

_____

8. What are some of the characteristics and philosophies you want the company you work for to have?

_____

_____

_____

_____

9. What specific steps can you take to improve your speaking, writing and intuitive skills?

_____

_____

_____

_____

Chapter 4
Prescriptions for
Comfort Management

SELF-ASSESSMENT

Before reading this chapter, rate yourself on the questions listed below.

How often do you feel stressed?

Not at all _____Most of the time

How often do you employ positive action during times of stress?

Never thought of it _____Always

How much control do you have over your own feelings?

None _____Total

How well do you deal with the stressful reactions of others?

I don't _____Completely

How well, overall, do you feel you cope with stress?

Poorly _____Very well

Prescriptions for Comfort Management

Oh, God,
why is all of this happening to me?

Grace,
everyone's family friend

We live in such a fast-paced society of competing demands, regardless of gender. Staying with the theme of Prosperity Thinking, the first success factor, I'd like to approach this chapter from the standpoint of looking at what provides comfort in your life. That's the fourth success factor: Prescriptions for Comfort Management.

If you have ever been asked to go to a stress management seminar, you probably became stressed thinking about the fact that you were going to be talking about what stresses you. So what you want to do is talk about what you need in your physical environment and what you need in your people environment that will give you the most comfort. You begin positioning yourself for success. We know that when we are in our comfort zone we think more clearly, we make better decisions, and we demonstrate our capabilities and skills in a more positive way than when we are stressed. We also know that when we are in our comfort zone, as opposed to being stressed, we take more time to think about the way that we word our communications. That strengthens Patterns for Power.

Do you see how the success factors all build upon each other? While you are in your comfort zone you can really focus on having optimal performance levels in each of the success factors including Programming for Play, Principle and Interest, and Purposing (which we will explore later).

Let's start by defining stress before you become too "comfortable"! Dr. Hans Selye, the grandfather of stress research, defined stress as "the body's physical, mental and chemical reactions to circumstances that frighten, excite, confuse, endanger or irritate you." Or, simply put, stress can be defined as your body's response to any real or imagined demand placed upon it.

Your body's initial response to stress is a chemical one. Chemicals are released into the body to prepare you to fight the situation or run from it. This chemical reaction causes heart and breathing rates to increase. In addition, blood pressure rises, muscles become tight, blood leaves the hands and feet and deposits in the large muscles, pupils dilate, and digestion ceases. All of these physical processes occur automatically (some occurring without our awareness) and prepare us for a "fight or flight" response.

Interestingly, this primitive response, which has allowed people to survive previous centuries, may be doing more harm than good in our current environment, unless stress is managed properly. The "fight or flight" response enables us to continue functioning efficiently during critical incidents or high stress situations. An example of this is coping with the sudden illness of a family member or participating in an athletic competition. Anyone who exists in a continual state of physical, emotional, or psychological stress is triggering these automatic chemical responses on a regular and recurring basis. Eventually, the mind and body must have relief from the stress or you will suffer negative side effects.

It is rarely appropriate for you literally to engage in "fight or flight" in your everyday environment and yet you activate this "fight or flight" response numerous times in the course of one day. This occurs as you respond to frustrations and environmental changes. You are not preparing for competition or survival, but the body has been placed on alert in anticipation of facing the current situation. According to Dr. Selye, if there is no way to adapt and the "fight or flight" reaction occurs too often, lasts too long, or is too intense, then stress-related diseases, illnesses and behaviors may begin to manifest in some of the following ways:

We may respond PHYSICALLY with:
- simple tension headaches
- migraine headaches
- back pain
- asthma
- allergies
- sexual impotence
- menstrual problems

- colitis
- ulcers
- high blood pressure
- coronary heart disease

We may respond PSYCHOLOGICALLY or emotionally with:

- worry
- fears
- anxiety and phobias
- lack of concentration
- frustration
- irritability
- quickness of temper
- depression
- feelings of isolation and helplessness

We may respond BEHAVIORALLY or interpersonally with:

- a loss or increase in appetite
- increased use of alcohol and drugs
- change in sleep habits
- change in sexual functioning
- increased sensitivity
- outbursts of inappropriate emotions or apathy

Another definition of stress that I hear frequently is "a feeling of being at a breaking point or feeling out of control." Not being in control of events and circumstances, not being in control of your own emotions, or not being able to control emotional outbursts of others can also impact your physical, psychological and behavioral states.

In the mid 1980s, the New England Journal of Medicine stated that 85 percent of all diseases and illnesses could be linked directly to personal or work stress. Only 15 percent were genetic or accident related. At the same time, The National Institute of Mental Health reported that 80 – 90% of industrial accidents and from 15 – 30% of employee absenteeism were related to stress.

More recently, The American Institute of Stress released the following: 60 – 80% of accidents on the job are stress-related and the double digit increases in workers' compensation premiums every year are due to mental stress claims. Also, survey results released by Integra reported that 65 percent of workers said that workplace stress had caused difficulties and more than 10 percent described these as having major effects; 10 percent said they work in an atmosphere where physical violence has occurred because of job stress; 29 percent had yelled at co-workers because of stress; 14 percent said machinery or equipment had been damaged because of workplace rage; and 2 percent admitted that they had actually struck someone.

These statistics raise the question as to why stress-related statistics haven't improved in the last twenty to thirty years. Is it because people aren't practicing comfort management activities? I don't think so. Most of those in my immediate circle of friends, family and colleagues are proactive in taking care of themselves; including involvement in physical exercise, positive nutritional regimens and various types of relaxation activities. It seems with all of the tools available to us, the pace and intensity of demands has increased proportionally with our education and training in comfort management.

In researching current stress-related data, there was so much information that it would be impossible to list all of the statistics. For you (S) and (C) types, go to the web and type in "stress studies" and you will find enough data to satisfy your appetite. For you (D) and (I) types, here's the bottom line: Personal and workplace stress is real and you must begin understanding your own stress tolerances, or lack thereof, and take control of your own reactions by employing comfort management activities before you can master Prescriptions for Comfort Management.

Not all stress is bad. Positive stress, or "eustress," can help you perform quickly and efficiently, can motivate you to concentrate more keenly, and can even propel you to new levels of performance. Some people claim they do their best work when they are stressed. Eustress is also manifested when you are excited about an anticipated event such as a new job, a new relationship, or even a new car. But just as with negative stress, you should not stay in a state of eustress for long periods of time. You should relax to build physical and emotional reserves that can be called upon when needed.

We begin to think that nothing short of moving to a deserted island can help. Stress is related to change and any change can cause it. Whether you suffer stress depends on how you look at the change that takes place: changing routines, changing partners, changing weather, changing diapers, changing lanes, or changing times. Even positive changes like falling in love, having children or getting a promotion can cause stress.

Oh, God, Why is All of This Happening to Me?

If the stress is severe and persistent, your immune system breaks down, your blood pressure rises, your spirits drop, and you end up in the hospital – like my friend Grace. Grace is the family friend who always had bad things happen to her. Her husband gambled away all their money, her kids were on drugs, lightning struck her house, and if that weren't enough, she had a car accident and ended up in the hospital with a broken leg. In the early hours of the morning, she looked up to the heavens and said, "Oh, God, why is all of this happening to me?" The thunder rolled and the clouds parted and a great voice boomed, "I don't know, Grace. There is just something about you that ticks me off!"

Do you ever feel like Grace? If you said yes, then you'll want to learn to control the stress in your life. Each person reacts differently to the impact of stress. But stress does not discriminate, anyone can experience it. ANYONE! Just as different events and relationships impact each of us in their own unique way, we all handle stress in our own way.

There are four ways to be resilient and creative in the face of stress:

1. Adopt a new perspective: refer to stress management as comfort management.

2. Be prepared for other people's and your own reaction to stress.

3. Employ positive actions during critical incidents.

4. Employ techniques to counteract negative physical impact.

Comfort Management

The first way to be resilient and creative in the face of excessive stress is to begin referring to stress management as "comfort management." In other words, put less emphasis on stress and more on comfort, and look at stress from a different perspective. Is that speaking euphemistically? Perhaps. But, by changing the focus from "stress" to "comfort," you are counteracting one perception with another, just as you did in the Posture of Excellence activity. You can learn to manage your life for maximum comfort.

Just as you can surround yourself with supportive personal and professional relationships, you can learn to position yourself for comfort management. Ask yourself, "What do I need in my physical and personal environments to give me the most comfort and to maintain my productivity?" How do you react to or perform under stress? What behavioral changes do you recognize in yourself? What behavioral changes can be seen by others when you are experiencing tension or stress?

Be Prepared

The second aspect of comfort management is knowing how you and others will behave in stressful situations, and being prepared for those reactions. It is not expecting people to do what you want; it's knowing how they will behave in a stressful situation. Let me say it another way. By knowing in advance how each style will likely react, you can be prepared to handle their responses productively rather than taking them personally.

There is a difference between tension and stress. Tension can be defined as moderate frustration. Stress, on the other hand, occurs when one's customary way of coping with tension is not effective. Stress often produces a change in our behavior. For example, a Dominant under moderate frustration (tension) may become demanding and autocratic. If the situation persists without resolution, that tension becomes stress, and a Dominant will avoid the situation or person causing the frustration.

Let's explore how each style reacts in situations of tension and stress.

When confronted, you may typically move from your comfort zone to tension. If you cannot resolve or counteract the cause of your tension, you may move to a high state of stress. But when your personal risks or investment is great enough, you may go directly from your comfort zone to a stressed state, bypassing tension. An example might be your reaction when a car fails to yield at a stop sign and crosses in the path of your car. You wouldn't say, "Oh, a car is running the stop sign. I must put on my brakes. Oh, gosh darn." You would most likely slam on your brakes, your heart rate would increase, and probably your temper, too , and you might shout out to the other driver and perhaps even show them an obscene gesture!

Style	Tension	High Stress
Dominant	Become demanding and autocratic	Avoid the situation or person causing the frustration
Influencer	Will go on the attack with negative feelings	Comply with those causing the frustration
Steady	Comply to maintain harmony	Attack as a method of returning to their comfort zone
Compliant	Avoid the person or situation to reduce frustration	Become autocratic, demanding that others comply

Study the "Reactions to Stress and Tension" chart. Based on what you perceive your own style to be, is this typical of your own tension and stress responses? Think of a recent conflict. Perhaps you had a disagreement with your boss, your partner, your spouse, or your child. You should be able to determine their primary interactive style. Recall how they responded in the conflict. How did you respond? Were your reactions similar to those described in the chart above?

Now, refer back to the chart to determine how the other person reacted. How would you adapt your own style now, knowing their reaction style? Knowing what to expect from your client, boss, employee, partner or spouse when they are in a tense or stressed states can make all the difference in maintaining a productive relationship. You do not take their reaction or response as a personal attack when you know that "it's just their style!" As a child, I am sure you quickly learned how to "read" your parents' moods before you asked for favors. You knew when they were in a good mood and when they weren't. You quickly made the decision, consciously or intuitively, when and how to ask for what you wanted. You can use your "people reading" skills when dealing with others to maintain more appropriate communications. With the information provided you can "read" the stress level of others and employ appropriate communications.

For example, if you know that your supervisor, colleague, or spouse is a (D) and goes into avoidance, then it is best to give them alone time. If you keep talking or interrupting them it will only exacerbate the situation and it will be difficult to reach agreement or concurrence on the issue. In other words, don't keep bugging them. If the person is a (C) then you can recognize that when they become autocratic and demanding, it is their way of coping. Don't be offended that they have forgotten pleasant greetings and "please" and "thank you." Being prepared for their behavior under tension and stress puts you in control. You are no longer allowing other people's stress to negatively impact you.

Employ Positive Actions

The third way to mange your comfort is to employ positive actions during critical incidents. Sometimes you're confronted with stress that you cannot avoid, such as illness, death or losing your job through no fault of your own. These are critical incidents. A critical incident is usually associated with significant changes or events. Critical incidents have a profound impact on you and may cause you to feel as if your life is out of control. At those times, you can regain control by taking action, some action, any action, to give you a sense of control over your life. Often, the most you can manage is to pick up a pencil. Something to do when there is nothing to be done. Writing down what you are experiencing forces you to focus on one thing, giving you relief from the confusion of the moment. Practice positive self-talk and write that self-talk down. Critical incidents can be catalysts for creative options. And one of the options is to find even the smallest positive from the incident and build from there.

Always try to think of something positive that can come out of a situation. The ability to cope is the relationship of the time-lapse between the crisis and the time when the situation is resolved and you are relaxed again. You can measure how you deal with the stress of a critical incident by that time-lapse. When you are in the midst of a critical incident, it is often difficult to identify your stressors or any positive outcome. At the moment of crisis, you need to try to project into the future and replace immediate feelings with those you think you'll be feeling after the crisis is resolved.

Most stress is not so dramatic. Day-to-day stress is more subtle. Sometimes you don't know that you feel bad until you feel better. Many of us are so used to body discomforts that we stop noticing them, just as we stop noticing habitual noises in our environment such as the noise of an airplane if we live near a flight path or the hourly chiming of a clock. It's a good idea to continually monitor your stress to alert you as to when you need to employ positive techniques to counteract negative physical impact, which is the fourth step in comfort management.

Employ Positive Techniques

There are several methods for exercising conscious control over stressful situations, relationships and feelings. Some of the most effective comfort management methods are presented. Select one that is compatible with your schedule and lifestyle. Remember to practice the same technique for several days so that you integrate the principles into your life. The method will then become a tool that can be employed whenever you need to move from a state of tension or stress back to your comfort zone. After you become proficient with one method, you may want to learn another method. Having several different techniques or tools available better prepares you to meet different types of stressful events, as well as allowing you to employ techniques that maintain your daily productivity and positive interpersonal relationships.

Autogenics and Progressive Relaxation allow you to locate areas of tension in the body and to release that tension by using specific verbal cues and relaxed breathing. Autogenics requires a concentration on a mental suggestion given to a specific body part or group of muscles. By concentrating on a specific suggestion such as "My right arm is heavy," you can actually feel your right arm getting heavier.

Progressive relaxation involves consciously tensing and consciously relaxing a specific body part or group of muscles. You learn to recognize the difference between the tensed state and the relaxed state. By increasing your awareness of the physical state of your body, you can more quickly take control.

In both autogenics and progressive relaxation, begin with one body part or muscle group and then move throughout the body, perhaps beginning with the arms, then moving on to the legs, back, abdomen, and so on. Each should be practiced for 10 to 15 minutes twice a day.

It is best to practice this technique in a quiet place with eyes closed and soft music playing in the background. By closing your eyes, visual distractions are eliminated. Soft music will help mask most distracting noises.

The **Posture of Excellence**, which incorporates visualization, is used to counteract stress with visual imagery. As we learned in Prosperity Thinking, it provides an opportunity to create mental pictures, whether real or imagined, that give you relief from the stress of the moment. You can visualize pleasant environments such as a beautiful island with white beaches and warm breezes or a mountain trail filled with the sounds of nature and the beauty of wild flowers. Note that visualization may include all of the senses: sight, sound, smell, touch or feeling. You may want to visualize a person or group of people with whom you have positive and supportive relationships. Affirm positive life experiences and the values and commitments that strengthen, protect and buffer you from stress.

Meditation is a practice that requires you to set aside time that is free from interruptions, a time for relaxing and contemplating. Meditation is not a religion, although most religions have a form of meditation incorporated into their practice. For maximum benefit, you should sit quietly with your eyes closed for 15 to 20 minutes twice a day. During your meditation, choose a word or phrase that is comfortable for you, such as a religious word or phrase, a mantra, a song title or any other word that has special meaning to you. You will repeat your word or phrase silently over and over to calm the mind and relax the physical body. A mantra is a word that is usually taken from an Eastern religion and is incorporated into various meditation practices. Those practicing a Western religion might not be comfortable using words from other religions, words whose meaning might not be understood. Just as with your cue word, select a word that will be natural for you.

Some call this time that is set aside their quiet time or prayer time or even "going to their cave." President Harry S. Truman said that he had a foxhole in his mind, a place where he could go to be unaffected by the external confusion. Tibetan llamas believe, unquestionably, that the most significant factor in our physical health is the state of our mind. Regardless of the descriptor or the specific words or phrases used, the practice of meditation has an important calming and centering effect necessary to feel in control of our lives emotionally and physically.

Use of Humor is an extremely effective intervention that can keep stress from building or can interrupt stress. The first step might be to find something to laugh about. Think about a joke you heard recently, a funny movie that you have seen, something amusing that happened to you. Force a laugh. If all else fails go to a funny movie, watch a comedy on television, or simply spend time with someone who can help create a light-hearted mood.

For nearly a decade, the Big Apple Circus Clown Care Unit at Babies and Children's Hospital of New York has been studying the impact of clowns during invasive procedures in pediatric oncology day clinics, and the effect of clowns on decreasing physiological and psychological distress in children and adolescents undergoing cardiac catheterization. The movie *Patch Adams* popularized the notion of clowning around with patients, especially children. Dr. Adam's goal of building the first "silly" hospital was for more than just entertainment. He saw it as a vital part of the medical treatment. Clowns at the Shriners Childrens Hospitals interact with their young patients by involving them in games and storytelling. Using humor helps overcome the trauma about hospital personnel, the medical equipment and procedures, and even the unfamiliar bed and hospital room. When the patients develop a positive attitude, it becomes a powerful partner in medical therapy.

Biofeedback is an extremely effective way to monitor physical states. Biofeedback allows you to monitor you own basic physiological functions. Functions that were previously thought to be involuntary, such as heart rate, blood pressure, body temperature and brain waves are some of these. Sensors are placed on the body to measure the level of skin moisture, muscle tension, or electrical activity. While practicing deep breathing and relaxation, a person receives one signal when their body process is achieving the desired result and a different signal when it isn't. The type of feedback given is varied. Some systems have headphones for auditory feedback, others have digital readouts for visual feedback, and still others provide a printout of the changes being produced in the body. Before attempting to use biofeedback, it would be best for you to consult an expert. There are many biofeedback specialists in private practice and in most major hospitals that can assist you in establishing current health baselines and then offer techniques that will be specific to your needs.

Hourly, Do Nothing! Every hour take a 10-minute break. The Hunza tribe in central Asia is considered by some to be the healthiest people in the world. It is believed that their practice of stopping hourly for about ten minutes to do nothing is the key factor. In many work environments, regulations call for workers to leave their work stations for a 10-minute break every hour. This is especially true for those who sit in front of computers, stand at a work station or are involved in repetitive tasks for long periods of time. A 10-minute break refreshes the mind and body. Perhaps we are positively modeling another culture's secret to wellness.

Physical Play is one of the best ways to reduce stress and contribute to overall improved health. This subject is so important, the next chapter will be devoted to it.

You may find it helpful to keep a log or journal of situations, people and events that stress you. Recognizing the stressors in your life enables you to design a plan to cope with the stress, to counteract the stress, or to correct the situation. Make an entry in the stress log each time you are aware of stress. Do this over a period of several days and take note of certain repetitive stressors. The following example from a stress log may assist you in designing your own format for recording your stress.

STRESS LOG FOR: (DAY)_____

STRESS #1:

Time: _____

Stressor (My stress comes from): _____

Who? _____

Where? _____

What? _____

I know that I'm stressed because (signs):

_____

_____

I usually adapt or resolve my stress by:_____

_____

In the future I will: _____

_____

Holding on to negative thoughts and feelings can manifest in physical problems. Just as positive thoughts manifest good feelings and outcomes, positive thoughts create good health. One of the best known examples of this is Norman Cousins, author of the classic, *Anatomy of an Illness*. Cousins changed a negative health diagnosis into a positive outcome by taking mental control of his illness. Believing that the effects of humor and laughter would contribute to the healing process, he repeatedly viewed old time comedy movies. He was able to turn his prognosis around and literally "laughed himself well!"

Let's reconstruct a stressful situation to see how you can make it more manageable and more controllable. You can't always change the outcome of a critical or stressful event, but you can change how you manage the stress related to the event. I'm going to ask you to recall a stressful event that has not yet been resolved satisfactorily, and give you an opportunity to see how you can cope with the stress related to that past negative experience. From previous chapters, you discovered that by repeating your cue word and assuming a Posture of Excellence, positive emotions can counteract negative emotions.

Thinking of ways a situation could have gone better or worse is a technique for coping with the past negative impact of a critical incident. It is important to realize that you can think of better ways to cope. Learn from it. If you're having trouble thinking of how the situation could have gone differently, or how it could have gone better, think of someone who handles problems well and try to model their behavior. Think of what they would have done in this situation. You may also find that in exploring different outcomes, you no longer want the outcome you had wanted at the time the incident occurred. But if you still do want it, spend a few moments and continue visualizing the outcome you desire.

Practice Application

Read the instructions completely so that you understand the practice application process. After you have done that, try it out!

- Get into a comfortable position with music playing softly in the background.
- Close your eyes.
- Take several deep breaths as you relax with the music.
- Now think about a negative situation, one that has not yet been resolved. When and where did it occur? What were you doing? Can you recall the emotions and feelings that you were experiencing in that situation and that you may still experience?
- Now imagine several possible endings. Think of ways the situation could have gone better. Now, think of ways the situation could have gone worse. Take a moment to do that now.

- If you did not get the outcome you wanted, and it is not possible to have it, remember a loss is sometimes a catalyst for change. It may free you to being open to experiences that you had been closed to before. Ask yourself, in looking back, if something positive came out of the experience. Did your life move in a new direction? Was there a new opportunity for growth? Was there a lesson learned during this experience? Although we may not understand at the time, we need to trust and believe everything happens for a reason. It may be months or even years before we truly understand the opportunity, the purpose or the lesson from a particular experience.

- I have had women say that they couldn't possibly think of anything positive that came from a situation or relationship that was still haunting them. Perhaps the most powerful lesson may simply be an awareness that they never want to be in that situation again! Awareness alone may prepare them and make them stronger for their future. It may add a new sense of control over their present lives.

- As soon as the past negative situation becomes vivid, repeat your cue word and assume your Posture of Excellence.

- Now recall a past fulfilling experience, a time when you received your desired outcome. This recollection is evidence to yourself that you've had fulfilling experiences in the past, and gives you confidence that you can have them again in the future. You are in control of your thoughts and feelings. You have counteracted one emotion with another. Being able to replace the negative situation with a positive one demonstrates your ability to control your thoughts and feelings.

- Silently repeat these or similar affirmations to reinforce this new positive feeling of being in control of your environment.

  ❖ *I am responsible for my thoughts.*

  ❖ *My feelings come from my thoughts.*

  ❖ *I am in control of my feelings.*

  ❖ *I am relaxed.*

  ❖ *I am calm.*

  ❖ *I am satisfied.*

  ❖ *I am content.*

  ❖ *I am feeling confident.*

  ❖ *I am capable.*

  ❖ *I am resilient and creative.*

- Remain relaxed with your eyes closed as you continue to feel confidently in control of your environment. Then, whenever you are ready, quietly and slowly stretch your arms and legs out in front of you, feeling energized and wide awake with renewed vitality.

Reinforcement Activities

1. How do you react to challenges, or to change? Describe the process you go through when you are confronted with unexpected change. Do you react differently to change that occurs in your home life versus your career?

   _____

   _____

2. Describe a critical incident in your life. How was it finally resolved? Looking back, what could you have done to help the situation at the time? Knowing that, what positive effect has it had on you and how could that information and knowledge be used in the future?

   _____

   _____

3. Describe the biggest risk you ever took in your life. Did you experience stress in making that decision? What was the outcome? How would you deal with the stress of risk-taking knowing what you know now?

   _____

   _____

4. What are your physical reactions to stress? What are you currently doing to prevent the physical problems caused by stress? What can you do in the future?

_____

_____

5. What are your psychological reactions to stress? What are you currently doing to prevent the psychological problems caused by stress? What can you do in the future?

_____

_____

6. What are your behavioral reactions to stress? What are you currently doing to prevent the behavioral problems caused by stress? What can you do in the future?

_____

_____

Chapter 5
Programming for Play

SELF-ASSESSMENT

Before reading this chapter, rate yourself on the questions listed below.

Have you ever used physical activity to help relieve stress?

Never _____Frequently

How much time do you devote to play each week?

None _____Lots

To what extent are you satisfied with your body?

Not at all _____Very satisfied

How often do you have a complete physical?

Never _____Once a year

How current are you on the research related to women's health issues?

Not at all _____Very Informed

Programming for Play

All work and no play makes Jill a . . .

Before we can talk about Programming for Play, we need to give some thought to energy. Energy is the foundation of your motivation, your inner beauty and your vitality. It is out there for the whole world to see. You must have energy of thought and motion to move forward in any endeavor – personally or professionally. Operating on low energy, or no energy at all, is like having a Ferrari with an empty gas tank. No matter how classy or beautiful on the outside, you can't run on empty. If you're dragging around a body that is always tired, you will not be perceived as being able to handle high-level responsibilities. You need to project the high-level energy expected of high performers.

As adults we've forgotten the therapeutic value of play. Physical play is a vital skill that can increase your energy; the same energy needed for your long-running performance. Many of you are so indoctrinated with the work ethic that you're unable to play or relax. Physical play was also mentioned in the previous chapter as an effective tool for reducing stress and managing your stress.

We are inundated with books, talk shows, videos and articles about diet and physical fitness do's and don'ts. I'm not advocating any particular nutrition or fitness regimen. What I am recommending is that your selection of any fitness or nutritional regimen be based on what is compatible with your lifestyle, your daily schedule, your interactive D.I.S.C. style, and the advice of your healthcare professional.

Play, as described in this chapter, includes physical activities and exercises that provide fitness benefits and contribute to overall physical and mental wellness. If you have trouble sticking with a fitness or exercise program, the reason may not be the work or the time involved. It may be that you have picked an activity that is not compatible with your preferred style. Also, find an activity that is fun. When you find an activity that is fun and feels natural, you are more likely to stick with it.

Approaches to a finish line are as varied as approaches to life. Each style has its own approach. Any activity can relate to any style depending on the motivation and desired outcome of the individual. Typically, if you are a (D), you probably want to participate in competitive sports such as racquetball, tennis, track and field. You also may be interested in activities that can boost the ego, such as weight lifting for a sleek, toned body. (D)s like recognition and awards for their efforts.

If you're an (I), social sports will appeal to you: aerobic dance and jazzercise, racquetball and tennis, anything that allows interaction with others. If you're an (I) and workout at home on an indoor trampoline, treadmill or other equipment, you may have to turn on the TV or radio for company. If you are an (I) and want to jog, get yourself a running mate to keep you company and to keep you motivated.

If you're an (S) you like social sports too, but you will prefer less competitive group activities. You will probably prefer bicycling or skating with a group, hiking clubs or folk dancing. An (S) may also like stay-at-home activities such as working out with a video program.

If you're a (C) you'll prefer more individual activities. You are more likely to choose activities that allow you to compete against your own record. You are the joggers, the cyclists and weightlifters. Your challenges are games of strategy – unfortunately, no one has yet figured out how to get an aerobic benefit from playing chess.

(D)s and (I)s can motivate themselves by envisioning the awards and recognition that they will receive. (I)s and (S)s like people-oriented activities. The (S) will want a structured sport and will stay with it forever, whereas (I)s will get everybody together and enthused, but may change sports with each new warm-up suit. Both (D)s and (C)s will participate with groups, but especially the (D), if she can be captain of the team. However, neither (D)s nor (C) really need a group.

As on any good team, you need all the players. You need the (D) to organize the team and be the captain. You need the (I) to get everyone motivated and to be the cheerleader. You need the (S) to comfort the losers. And you need the (C) to keep score and referee, as she's the one who knows all the rules.

Our strenuous play does not have to stop as we get older. Medical authorities say we are capable of continuing to do whatever we did in our prime, only a little slower. Those who take time out for play and physical activity find it increases their overall stamina and mental awareness.

It seems that there aren't enough hours in the day and then we are supposed to find time to play? It's a matter of setting priorities. If you're dragging around a body that's not physically sound, you will not be as productive and useful to your organization, your family or yourself. You may want to start by walking to develop confidence in yourself that you can do some activity. An added benefit is that these activities burn calories, aiding in weight reduction, if that is one of your concerns. Always check with your physician and get recommendations before beginning a physical exercise program, be it formal or informal.

Patience Hell, I Want to Kill Something!

There are health issues that should be of paramount concern to all women as they can prevent you from participating in any physical activity or maintaining optimal on-the-job performance. They are related to hormone levels and the resulting impact on your body, energy level, mood and coping skills. Some of the issues may include premenstrual syndrome (PMS), osteoporosis and pre- and post-menopause.

PMS

I will mention PMS only briefly, but PMS is a legitimate health problem for some women. PMS is a physiological condition accompanied by headaches, nausea, aching joints, and water retention, but we usually hear more about the emotional side effects such as irritability, fatigue, mood swings, increased sensitivity and crying easily.

Nutritional supplements, hormone treatments, reducing stress in your daily routine, and being physically active are some interventions that can alleviate the symptoms. Relaxation techniques such as meditation, yoga and biofeedback are especially helpful in controlling the stress related to PMS. If you suspect that you may suffer from PMS, consult you physician.

Not all women are affected by changes in emotions and behaviors during monthly pre-menstruation but the negative stereotype that all women will have behaviors related to PMS has impacted the view of women in the workplace. Many believe that women are less able to handle the pressures of job responsibilities and personal interactions because they are suffering PMS. It is important to identify and understand the impact of PMS on your personal attitudes, emotions and behaviors. By identifying this impact, change agents can be employed to minimize any negative impact on your productivity and the professional image that you project.

Overcoming the Negative Stereotype of PMS

Many women reinforce this negative stereotype by verbalizing (making excuses for attitudes and behaviors) by saying to others that they must be suffering PMS. Joining in when others make jokes about PMS only perpetuates this stereotype. Using the Posture of Excellence skill is an effective way to maintain a positive and controlled attitude during PMS. Not participating in workplace jokes and comments about PMS can counteract the power that this stereotype has had over the perception of women's abilities.

Osteoporosis

Osteoporosis is another health concern – especially for women. Osteoporosis is a thinning and weakening of the bones and is insidious because it is a silent disease. We don't know we have it until it's too late to take preventive steps. Osteoporosis affects one out of every four women. Over one million bone fractures a year are linked to osteoporosis. The complication related to hip fractures is the twelfth leading cause of death in the United States.

Fortunately, much attention and research has led to better education and awareness of osteoporosis. It is not a new disease. The fact is, all of us probably know someone who has suffered from it, a grandmother, an aunt, or an older woman we knew who suffered a fall, broke a hip or became bedridden. Often the complications, like pneumonia, were fatal. We just thought it was old age or didn't connect it to the real cause. We didn't know it was a disease, we didn't know it was preventable, and we usually didn't associate it with younger women. It can begin as early as puberty, and certainly begins by age 35. Although symptoms may not appear until 20 years later, prevention should begin in our mid-thirties.

Osteoporosis occurs mostly in women after menopause, when a woman's ovaries stop producing estrogen. In fact, one-third of a woman's lifetime bone loss can occur in the first five years following menopause. A hysterectomy and removal of both ovaries also increases your risk of developing osteoporosis. Women who stop menstruating for a prolonged time due to anorexia, bulimia or excessive physical exercise may lose bone mass. Bone loss can cause bones to become thin, weak, and more likely to fracture. The disease can result in severe back pain, dowager's hump, fractured bones and shortened height. Bones can become so fragile and brittle that they break under pressure as slight as opening a sealed jar.

There are many factors that determine who will develop osteoporosis. The first step in prevention is to determine whether you are at risk. Although you may look and feel fine, you could be at risk for osteoporosis and not know it. If you think you are at risk, if you are post-menopausal or have a family history of osteoporosis, talk to your doctor and ask whether a bone mineral density (BMD) test may be right for you. A BMD determines the health of your bones and can establish a baseline for continual monitoring.

Calcium deficiency – Throughout a woman's life, calcium and vitamin D play a key role in maintaining bone health. It's not just insufficient calcium intake, but a reduction of the body's ability to absorb calcium that causes the deficiency. Proportional intake of vitamin D has been indicated as necessary for better calcium absorption.

Lack of regular exercise – Inactivity makes your bones lose strength and become thinner. Over time, thin bones may break. Women who aren't active are at increased risk of osteoporosis. Exercises, such as walking and jogging, that pull and stress the long bones are the best for women.

Gender – Women are eight times more likely to develop osteoporosis than men because men have greater bone and muscle mass.

Genetic factors – Caucasian and Asian women seem to be more at risk than African American women

Smoking – Women who smoke have increased calcium excretion and have been shown to have less bone mass than non-smokers. In addition, nicotine causes blood vessels to constrict and become narrower, leaving less room in the bloodstream for bone-building nutrients.

Medications used in the treatment of certain conditions – A significant, and often overlooked, risk factor in the development of osteoporosis is the use of certain medications to treat chronic medical conditions.

Medications used to treat rheumatoid arthritis, underactive thyroid, seizure disorders, and gastrointestinal disorders may have side effects that can increase bone loss and lead to osteoporosis. Corticosteroids (e.g. for asthma or arthritis), thyroid hormones or blood thinning medications are just a few types of these medications, so you may want to check with your doctor to see if any of these have bone loss side effects. For many people, these are life-saving or life-enhancing drugs. That is why it is important to discuss the use of these medications with your doctor and not stop or alter your medication dose on your own.

Although there is no cure for osteoporosis, preventive measures are available. Only you and your physician can determine which one is best for you. Most of us can prevent osteoporosis through:

- Increased calcium intake.
- Estrogen replacement therapy.
- Exercise.
- Consulting with a physician to determine your risks, current bone mass levels, and any preventive treatments you may require.

Increased Calcium Intake – Bone tissue is always growing and changing, but after age thirty-five, and especially after menopause, bone loss accelerates. Women who approach menopause with low calcium reserves and a sedentary lifestyle are especially at risk, as are dieters, since calorie counting often eliminates calcium-rich foods.

You can take calcium in tablet form instead of or in addition to eating calcium-rich foods. You should check with your doctor on the supplemental amount, but the general recommendation is 1000 milligrams a day for those under fifty years of age and 1200 milligrams a day for those over fifty. Become more aware of the nutritional value of what you are eating (vitamins, minerals, sodium content and calories, etc.). Although adding calcium-rich foods to your diet can certainly help prevent osteoporosis, it would take eight or nine cups of broccoli (one cup = 136 mg of calcium) to reach the suggested daily intake of calcium.

Listed below are foods that have been shown to be high in calcium content. Which of the following foods are you eating on a regular basis (at least three times a week)?

Almonds	Lowfat or skim milk
Barley	Milk
Broccoli	Oranges
Buckwheat	Parsley
Buttermilk	Pecans
Cabbage	Romaine lettuce
Celery	Rutabaga
Cheese	Sardines
Collard greens	Sesame seeds
Cottage cheese	Spinach
Dry beans	Sprouts
Globe artichokes	Turnip greens
Green beans	Watercress
Kale	Yogurt

Hormone Replacement Therapy – Another preventive measure for osteoporosis is hormone replacement therapy (HRT). The onset of menopause accelerates the potential hazards of osteoporosis as estrogen production drops dramatically. Estrogen has been found to be critical in maintaining bone calcification. When estrogen levels drop, bones dissolve at a greater rate than calcification, causing them to become weak and fragile. Much controversy surrounds hormone replacement therapy. Some studies have linked hormone replacement therapy with an increased chance of some types of cancer, while other studies contradict such findings. Each woman must weigh the benefits and risks of all of her health choices including whether or not to use hormone replacement therapy in bone loss prevention.

Exercise – In addition to increasing your calcium intake or possible hormone replacement therapy, exercise is vital in preventing osteoporosis. A study at the University of Wisconsin found that 30 minutes of exercise three times a week not only prevented bone loss, but produced a gradual increase in bone strength and mineral content. The muscular pull on the bones and regularly putting weight on them helps maintain bone tissue. Jogging, race-walking and biking are the best activities for maintaining healthy bones. Pressure applied to the bones in those activities is enough to stimulate bones to absorb and deposit more calcium from the blood.

One of the earliest studies of astronauts confined to a gravity-free spacecraft for eight days found the astronauts lost 200 milligrams of calcium a day. Despite cleverly designed exercise programs, the absence of gravity in space made it impossible to put pressure on the bones, so bones began to lose calcium until gravity was restored and walking and lifting were resumed.

Ask you doctor about a test to evaluate your bone density. Ideally, find an activity that provides both stress on the bones plus aerobic benefit, one that gets your heart rate up to the appropriate level for your age for 20 minutes, three times a week. If you've been inactive, ask your physician for your specific desired heart rate but the following chart can serve as a guide. Most health related information advises that your maximum heart rate should be 220 minus your age, that you include a slow warm up of 5 – 10 minutes, gentle stretching, a gradual climb to your target heart rate

Age* (in years)	Target Heart Rate (50% – 85%)#		Average Maximum Heart Rate (100%)#
20	100	170	200
25	98	166	195
30	95	162	190
35	93	157	185
40	90	153	180
45	88	149	175
50	85	145	170
55	83	140	165
60	80	136	160
65	78	132	155
70	75	128	150

* in years
\# in beats per minute (BPM)

range, and then ending with a 5 – 10 minutes of cool down and stretching.

You might note that I didn't include swimming in the above recommendations. Although it's a good aerobic activity, it has little benefit for preventing bone loss because there is no pressure on bones when suspended in water. Swimmers may want to add activities that put pull on the bone.

Walking just nine miles a week decreases your chances of osteoporosis. If you are a little more adventurous, try race-walking over jogging. You know, that funny looking fast walking. Actually, I discovered race-walking when the elastic in my panty hose gave way while I was running to catch a plane. Race-walking takes longer to get the same aerobic benefit as jogging, but it's less jarring on the joints. It's also more effective for losing waistline inches. It's the ideal sport for those just beginning a new program and for older women. All race-walking really requires is a good pair of shoes and a nonchalant, thumb-your-nose attitude towards passers-by who may give you a questioning smile.

The added demands of balancing career and home can interfere with implementing or maintaining a proper physical fitness program. At the end of the chapter is a chart that will assist you in determining how much time per week you can devote to your physical fitness routine, as well as who you need to coordinate with to accomplish this goal.

Travel can take its toll on a fitness routine. If you cannot locate a hotel with an exercise room, take along a favorite workout CD or DVD and do an aerobic exercise routine in the hotel room. Some other alternatives include:

- Rent a bicycle. One day while I was in Adelaide, Australia, my client and I rented bicycles and toured the city. It was wonderful to interact on a more personal way with the local environment and visit with those we met along the way. I can't think of a better way to see a new and exciting city.
- If you are a member of a health spa, get a listing of its affiliates.
- If you are visiting friends or a business associate make arrangements to be their guest at their health spa or schedule a game of racquetball or tennis with them.
- If you enjoy walking, visit a local mall, especially if you are unsure of the safety of walking in the area where you are staying. Take a stroll in a local park or along a scenic path in the city.
- Check out a local ice skating or roller-skating rink.
- When traveling with an associate, work out together. You may take advantage of fitness activities if you have someone to go with you.
- If you have a flight layover, take advantage of the time by walking around the terminal. I travel in comfortable clothes and walking shoes whenever possible.

It is estimated that about one-half of us suffer our first humiliation in life in athletics. But, I do believe that each of us can play a pretty good game of something. Just remember the rule, TRAIN, DON'T STRAIN! If the idea of starting a physical fitness program is pulling you out of your comfort zone, why not start with some stretching exercises or some simple activities that you can do at home or during the lunch hour.

Consult a Physician – As I have mentioned several times, you should consult your physician or other health care provider before making any decisions about nutrition, medications or exercise. A family history of specific health concerns can also impact attitudes and behaviors. When a family is prone to a specific health concern, it may cause individuals to focus on the possible negative outcomes in their life. Knowing what tendencies have affected other family members can be a catalyst for action to prevent that same condition in your life. Staying current on research and interventions that have been effective can prepare you to take actions to prevent or alleviate negative side effects. This puts you in control of your physical wellness instead of keeping you in a victim state.

Food, Glorious Food!

If you feel that you aren't eating right or that your illness may be related to your diet, one suggestion is to keep a food diary for at least two weeks. Keep track of all intake, be it water, vitamins, or other supplements. Write down what you ate, the time you ate it, and the amount.

Keeping a food diary helps you become aware of what you are eating. It also helps you see patterns of behavior. For example, after a week of keeping a food diary, you may learn that every day between 3:30 p.m. and 4:00 p.m., you tend to reach for the snacks. You may also notice that you are only drinking one or two glasses of water a day and the rest of the time you drink coffee or a diet beverage.

All of this information will help you to understand your own tendencies, and if you should decide to seek advice from a nutritionist, she will be able to more quickly assess your current condition. It may also provide additional data if you plan to reduce your caloric intake.

Practice Application

Remember to reinforce your commitment to physical wellness by repeating these or similar affirmations:

❖ *I am becoming healthier and stronger each day.*

❖ *I am experiencing renewed energy.*

❖ *I am physically fit.*

❖ *I am enjoying my daily exercise.*

❖ *I am eating healthy, nutritious foods.*

❖ *I am participating in aerobic activities three times a week.*

❖ *I am aware of current health issues that may affect me.*

Whatever you do remember to have FUN!

Reinforcement Activities

1. How many hours per week can you commit to physical play? Shade in the spaces that are already filled with daily activities, work, hobbies, shopping, etc.

This simple graph will give you a better idea of your current scheduling. Once you have shaded in your committed time, you can then look at your discretionary time. This time could be used for play even if it's only half of the square (30 minutes), that's a start! If your day starts other than 6 a.m., shift the numbers on the chart.

Your typical day

	6 a.m.	7 a.m.	8 a.m.	9 a.m.	10 a.m.	11 a.m.	12 p.m.	1 p.m.	2 p.m.
Sunday									
Monday									
Tuesday									
Wednesday									
Thursday									
Friday									
Saturday									
	3 p.m.	4 p.m.	5 p.m.	6 p.m.	7 p.m.	8 p.m.	9 p.m.	10 p.m.	11 p.m.
Sunday									
Monday									
Tuesday									
Wednesday									
Thursday									
Friday									
Saturday									

2. What would you like to change about your current physical lifestyle that would allow you to incorporate more play into your life? What sports have you previously been involved in? Were they fun? What

117

sports sound most appealing to you right now? How could they be incorporated into your schedule?

3. There are health concerns that affect women. Prevention, monitoring and early detection can help keep you healthy and active.

When was your last Ob/gyn examination?

_____

When was your last complete physical?

_____

When was your last mammogram?

_____

When was your last bone mineral density test?

_____

Chapter 6
Principal and Interest

SELF-ASSESSMENT

Before reading this chapter, rate yourself on the questions listed below.

Are you making as much money as you'd like?

Are you kidding _____Absolutely

How comfortable are you around financially successful people?

Miserable _____In my element

Do you feel you are in control of your money?

Not at all _____Absolutely

How often do you think of image improvement as an investment?

Not at all _____Often

Are you projecting an image that attracts success?

Not at all _____Absolutely

Are you currently utilizing your financial resources to their fullest potential?

Not at all _____To the maximum

Principal and Interest

Respecting your relationship with money, you see,
is the key not only to your security and independence,
but to your happiness as well.

Suze Orman

In Prosperity Thinking, we talked about the abundance of wealth available to us, and defined abundance as warmth and safety, privacy and comfort, ease and luxury, and opportunities for advancement. Let's bypass these euphemistic words. Let's talk about MONEY. Money is an emotional issue. It impacts relationships within marriages, personal and business partnerships, and your relationship with yourself. It is often considered taboo to talk about and yet money is a major part of everyone's life.

You are not liberated in any sense until you are where you want to be economically. Money has an important purpose in your life. First and last, it should help you achieve what you want, personally and professionally. Money should provide self-reliance and independence. Any other use of money is a waste. Now there's an idealistic statement for you. Too bad your landlord, plumber, grocer, and kids' orthodontist don't subscribe to it. Of course, you have obligations, but once your rent is paid, the groceries are on the table, your car's gas tank is full, and your children's teeth are straightened, you need to focus on short- and long-term financial goals.

At this point, I would like to interject that I do not mean that the accumulation of personal wealth is the meaning of life. I do not subscribe to the theory, "She who has the most toys when she dies, wins." There are certainly altruistic virtues that supersede hedonistic ones, and remembering to give to others may be a contributing factor in your feeling of success. What is really meant by "money should, first and last, help you achieve what you want, personally and professionally," is that, after the obvious obligations are taken care of, remember your obligation to yourself. Money should provide the resources for your lifetime development, and lifetime development should be your first priority. Getting or having money itself is not the objective; it's what you do with the money once you have it.

There is a certain freedom that comes from having money available to us. And that freedom is important in our lives. Joe Louis said, "I'm not crazy about money, but having it quiets my nerves." I can relate to that. But getting money in the bank is the starting point. And that comes from developing Prosperity Thinking as an everyday habit. Too many of us have operated on the principle of scarcity thinking. Scarcity thinking is focusing on what we lack. We've all heard the expression, "looking at the glass as half full instead of half empty." Scarcity thinking is seeing the glass half empty.

If talking about money is uncomfortable for you, it may be that you were programmed that women didn't talk about money or that you don't feel you successfully handle your money matters, which may relate to shame, guilt or anxiety.

From PIN Number to Panic!

Shelly (no, that's not her real name) a close friend of mine, was an overspender. Shelly was constantly shopping and buying unneeded items because they were on sale, because they were the latest fad, or to give to friends and family for special occasions such as a birthday or simply because they dropped in on a Wednesday afternoon. She then spent her energy hiding her spending from her husband; finding new places to hide these items and explaining them when they were brought out in the open. She told me, and I am sure others, how she rushed home to get the mail so her husband wouldn't see the credit card bills, which was a constant energy robber. She may have seen the buying as an energy giver, but that energy was quickly replaced by fear!

Shelly readily admits that her spending was almost addictive and that she learned that her behavior stemmed from growing up in a home where money was so tight that she and her five siblings never got toys for birthdays or Christmas. They usually got new underwear and a pair of shoes that would have to last until the next birthday or Christmas. She remembers poring over page after page in magazines and catalogs, visualizing herself in the latest fashions and giving extravagant presents to others. As an adult, she was very successful in her position as a sales representative and her monthly commissions, not even including her base pay, far exceeded her family's yearly income. She could now open to any page in a magazine or catalog and have the money to buy what she saw. AND SHE DID! The awareness of her money motivations became a tool for her to begin to understand how she could use her income in different ways, including putting money aside for retirement, and still satisfy an emotional need related to money. Shelly told me recently that it is still a constant struggle but she has learned to counteract the urge to go shopping with swimming. When she has the uncontrollable urge to get in her car and go shopping, she drives to a local health club and swims for an hour. She reminds herself that she is doing something healthy for her physical body and contributing to her financial health.

Much of your attitude (values) toward and interest in money matters may have been shaped as you were growing up. For some of you it may have been a lack of role models, especially female role models, in financial matters. Your attitudes may be based on the attitudes of your parents, other significant adults, your geographic area's economy or cultural influences.

- What are your attitudes toward money?
- How did your mother and father regard money?
- What programming are you living with that may be preventing you from achieving prosperity?
- What programming are you living with that reinforces that you are completely worthy of a prosperous life?

In past years, few women were involved in major financial matters. Handling financial matters had traditionally been left to men. Subconsciously, many women may still find it difficult to relate to earning and managing large amounts of money if earlier experiences reinforced that men were primarily responsible for financial decisions or that women didn't make significant financial decisions without checking with a man to get his okay. Some women treat money as if it's an acquired taste. Getting used to the idea of financial abundance shouldn't have to be an acquired taste. Women should take to it immediately.

Remember that your learned beliefs may have included the idea that women shouldn't manipulate or handle large amounts of money. Yet women have a natural affinity for finances. Women have traditionally handled the household budget. Moving beyond smaller budget items from groceries and lunch money to the larger financial decisions, such as whether to buy the boat, the investment property or the blue-chip stocks, is not a big leap. The skills required for identifying financial needs, determining where and how you will generate needed funds, and allocating funds appropriately can be learned. Relying on someone else to make financial decisions for you gives away your ability to control your future. Remember, a lack of experience or confidence doesn't mean a lack of competence!

Protecting Paula?

Even today women share with me stories about being denied credit, including credit cards, personal loans and home loans. Paula, a single woman who was earning nearly six figures, wanted to buy a house that would be easily affordable on her salary. Her story was almost identical to one that I was told more than 20 years ago! When Paula went to her bank – the same bank where she had kept her savings and checking accounts for years – her loan application was denied. The loan officer openly told her that the reason was that they needed to "protect women," even though her salary was more than sufficient to meet the payments. Because women didn't understand money matters, a male would have to sign her application, demonstrating that he had explained all details of the transaction to her. He could also ensure that she made timely payments. Paula said that she was furious, but didn't know what else to do. It was the perfect house; the price was right; it was a smart financial move to quit paying rent and start building equity in a house; and time was of the essence if she was going to be able to make an offer on the house before someone else did. She didn't know how to fight the system so she asked a male friend to co-sign for her. Within a few months and with the advice of a financial planner, she refinanced her house with no co-signer! Now, in looking back at this event, she says, "Why protect me? Educate me so I can protect myself! And by the way, educate lenders that women are fiscally responsible on their own!" Now that leads to asking, have we come a long way, baby, when it comes to being recognized as financially savvy and fiscally responsible? Hmmm, guess I would have to say we're not there yet.

We're In It for the Long Haul

Women are major players in the workforce and have come a long way in nontraditional jobs, holding political positions and moving into senior leadership roles. In 2006, the AFL-CIO reported that 40 percent of working women worked evenings, nights or weekends, 38 percent earned all or almost all of their family's income and 20 percent worked two or more jobs. There are as many statistics as there are sources on women and money and every woman's situation is unique; however, the following are statistics to consider when learning to "educate and protect" yourself as Paula declared.

- 12 percent of women 65 and older are in the workforce (Bureau of Labor Statistics).
- 12 percent of women 65 and older were living in poverty compared with 7 percent of men in 2005 (U.S. Census Bureau). Notice any similarity to the first bullet?
- The average age of widowhood is 55 to 58.
- In 2004, only 40 percent of women 62 and older received Social Security benefits based solely on their own earnings, the same as in 1960 and only 40 percent over 55 were eligible for a pension, compared to 53 percent of men (Center for Retirement Research).
- Newly retired men receive Social Security checks that are 47 percent larger than those for women (*Dayton Daily News*).
- Women average $11\frac{1}{2}$ years out of the workforce.
- 70 percent of pre-retirement income will be needed for retirement.
- 40 percent of first marriages and 50 percent of all marriages will end in divorce.
- 60 percent of women didn't know how a mutual fund worked compared to 41 percent of men; 60

percent of women are more likely to pay the bills; 67 percent of women balance the checkbook and 54 percent maintain the family budget, while only 25 percent of women versus 44 percent of men reported they were responsible for buying and selling stocks, bonds and mutual funds (OppenheimerFunds survey).

- 2 out of 3 working women earn less that $30,000 per year and 9 out of 10 working women earn less than $50,000 per year (Women's Institute for a Secure Retirement).

- The earnings gap among recent women college graduates appears the first year and widens over the next 10 years (American Association of University Women).

McKenna's Story, the Good News

It is not all doom and gloom on the financial horizon for women. McKenna Stephens, financial advisor, gives her take on women and their money. I have known McKenna Stephens for several years and have often heard her speak with sincerity and conviction as to how women must take control of their finances. In age she could be my daughter, but in wisdom she is wiser by many years. She gives some important statistics and shares a critical significant event that led her to a successful career as a financial advisor.

One of the greatest motivators for me in educating women about their money is the fact that I have seen what can happen when you don't take the time to plan. It happened in my own family. I grew up in such an amazing family – my sister and I had two parents who loved us and each other so much. After my sister and I went to college, my parents had the opportunity to do things for themselves, and while retirement wasn't something in the near future, they had started saving and were excited about the future.

Then the unthinkable happened, my father, at the young age of 54, was diagnosed with terminal lung cancer. He passed away four months later. This left my mom with her income cut in half, but the same level of expenses. And they didn't have enough life insurance. It's not that my Dad didn't care, they just didn't know. No one ever took the time to really talk to my parents about life insurance or retirement planning. If they had, perhaps my mom wouldn't have to work as hard as she does today.

That's why it is imperative that you don't wait. Get involved in your finances! Start today!

Today, more than ever, women are a driving force in the economy. In fact, American women make up the largest economic force in the world, spending $9.4 trillion per year. And we are making strides not only as consumers, but in business as well. Consider the following statistics:

- *Women represent 47 percent of the workforce.*
- *In the 2005-2006 school year, women will earn 59 percent of the bachelor's degrees and 60 percent of the master's degrees.*
- *Women own an estimated 10.6 million firms, which generate over $2.5 trillion in sales.*
- *By 2010, women are expected to acquire 94 percent of the growth in U.S. private wealth.*

It is evident that women have become a powerful force in today's society; economically, academically, professionally and personally. However, there are certain truths that affect women and are, in turn, the drivers behind the particular financial issues we need to consider.

- *Women still earn less – 79 cents for each dollar men earn*
- *Women are more likely to spend time away from work to care for a child or a parent, in comparison with men*
- *Women earn lower social security benefits*
- *Women can expect to live almost six years longer than men*

At first glance, these facts may seem nothing more than numbers. Perhaps a reminder that we should be doing something, but not necessarily a motivator to get started. However, if you really take the time to think about these statistics, most people will realize that either they or someone close to them has been affected by one of these situations. And the outcome may not have been ideal.

This first thing you need to do is evaluate your current situation. Set clear, concise, realistic goals for your future. Where do you see yourself personally and professionally in the next 5, 10 and 20 years? If you don't know where you are going, how can you possibly choose a strategy to get there?

Once you have set these goals, get help in devising an investment strategy that takes into account your risk tolerance and time horizon. And be sure to pay yourself first. Treat your investments like a bill that must be paid every month.

You Know Radar O'Reilly?

I still remember when Radar O'Reilly, a mythical male came to my rescue. For those who remember the sitcom

M.A.S.H., Radar was from Ottumwa, Iowa, my home town. I was in a discount store in a small town in Kansas many years ago when I discovered at the cash register that I didn't have enough cash to pay for my purchase. So I wrote out a check and handed it to the cashier. She looked at it and asked very quizzically, "Where is Ottumwa, Iowa?" Behind me, I heard someone ask, "Who's from Ottumwa, Iowa? Do you know Radar O'Reilly?" Two people in back of her said, "Radar O'Reilly? You know Radar?" The cashier took one look at me and said, "You know Radar O'Reilly?" She initialed the check and let me on my way, forgetting that she had asked for my picture ID.

Suicide or Security?

Women are no longer leaving their financial decisions in the hands of others, men or women. They have taken control of their future by successfully managing their personal resources. If you want to avoid financial suicide, you need to take control of your own money matters. It is not a question of whether you should get involved; it is a question of how to overcome old spoken or unspoken rules about your involvement. The more you educate yourself on money matters, the more prepared you are to manage your finances and the more easily you will be accepted into the financial world of your profession.

Today, just as it was twenty years ago, there is still a difference in the way men and women are briefed as new employees during their on-the-job orientation. New male employees are given a more in-depth look at the financial structure of the organization; whereas, women are given detailed information on the personnel structure. Men, more than women, were usually seen as the ones who would move into jobs that required financial awareness. While there doesn't seem to be deliberate gender discrimination, there still is the perception of the career paths that men and women will take.

There's a lot of financial information available for someone willing to learn. Here are some hints to get you going.

Financial Fitness

Take financial classes – These classes are often offered free by brokerage houses. They are usually an enticement to get you to invest your nest egg with that company, so be aware they may try to pressure you to buy. Attend a number of lectures and seminars while you're learning. Then, choose a broker whom you feel is knowledgeable and whose style seems compatible with yours.

Read financial books and magazines – Read the financial pages of your newspaper. Even if they don't make sense to you at first, keep reading. Also, watch financial shows on television.

Find a mentor – This can be a friend or colleague, a broker, or anyone who is knowledgeable and loves to talk about investing. A good way to learn the game is to explore how your own profession is affected by Wall Street. To some extent, we are all involved, whether we know it or not.

Consult a financial planner – Interview several financial planners to determine their ability to meet your needs before hiring one. Make sure that you choose one with whom you will be comfortable.

After you've educated yourself and feel comfortable about investing, you may want to start small. Just as you wouldn't buy racing skis as a beginner on the bunny slope, buy a few shares of a very low-cost stock. This is an opportunity to learn about buying and selling stocks without risking too much. You may want to join an investment club where several people put in a small amount and jointly invest. Learning about money gives you the courage to adopt a more aggressive stance.

If you are investing in real estate, you may want to find a partner to minimize your initial risk. There are many excellent evening and weekend courses that offer detailed strategic plans for purchasing investment property. They outline, step-by-step, what is required, from determining the initial location of the property to the recommendations on how to protect your investment. Real estate investments often become less liquid in hard times. Knowing this, you may want to diversify your investments.

Some advice I received in a financial planning class has always stayed with me. You should only invest the amount you can afford to lose. That means only invest the amount that you can lose without jeopardizing your current standard of living or obligations. No matter what you invest in, be it stocks or bonds, real estate or business opportunities, the same rules apply. Educate yourself, start small and use money multipliers.

In order to multiply your efforts resulting in increased earnings, your financial involvements could include money multipliers such as partners, investors and money advisors such as your financial planner, lawyer, banker or accountant. Exclude all others from your money dealings, no matter how well-meaning they may be. I remember some early advice that my accountant gave me, which was to never, ever talk about money issues with anyone who doesn't have a specific reason for knowing! Hmmm, no problem. The only time I talked about money was when I didn't have any, which was most of the time when I first started my business. I was reminded that I was creating an image that I wasn't skilled enough to run a business if I was constantly talked about a shortage of cash flow.

Since then I have realized that the women I knew just didn't talk about their finances, except when they were talking about not having money or about their own lack of control over using what money they did have. When my business began flourishing with large consulting contracts and the popularity of my training videos and book, I found that I had been catapulted into a different level of success. I wanted to tell the whole world that my business was doing well but found that, instead, I would still engage in conversations about the lack of money. Old habits don't die quickly. I had grown up with the constant warning that you did not brag. Not that I wanted to brag to make others feel less fortunate but I just wanted people to know that I had a vision of being a successful business owner and that I was achieving my dream. I found the balance by knowing with whom I could share my successes. I would not be seen as a braggart but as a friend who was excited about a positive aspect of my life. Interestingly, these were the same people who encouraged me to go for my dream and seemed to feel they were a part of my success.

Another financial strategy is to have continuing returns from one effort. Some advice that hit home with me was when a successful author friend, Denis Waitley, said to me, "Whatever your investment, it should make money even while you sleep. I know while I'm sleeping, somewhere in the world, someone is buying my book." Can you think of money-multiplying techniques that will enhance your efforts?

After investing, monitor your investment personally. No one is going to care about your investments as much as you do. Read newspapers and magazines to find out what is happening in the industry in which you have invested. Consult your broker periodically to get recommendations. Finally, review your financial goals regularly.

The following principles may assist you in defining your financial goals:

1. Make flexible financial decisions. To do this you should select assets and investments that are easily sold (liquid). That will enable you to respond to any changes that occur in the market.

2. At certain stages, build a cash surplus to finance later periods of your life. There's a time to save and a time to spend, and our needs change with age. After basic necessities, that surplus will support your personal development.

3. Keep money decisions personal. Keep your financial goals aligned with your personal development. Review your financial goals as you make investment decisions.

An important aspect of keeping your financial development aligned with your personal development is to invest in your image. Robert Pante, in *Dressing to Win*, said abundance begins with dressing ourselves as if we already had wealth, because that changes our self-image to one of deserving. He claimed if you dress well, really well, good things start to come your way, "automatically, inevitably, like falling dominoes."

This Looks Like a Housewife from Boise, Idaho!

Just as the easiest way to get a loan is to prove you don't need it, the quickest way to be recognized and accepted as successful is to look like you already have achieved success. Dressing with style and class is a catalyst that causes miraculous changes in your life. Pante's philosophy was simple and logical. He said dressing well meant looking better. Looking better makes you feel better about yourself and when you feel better about yourself you project a more confident image. This self-assured, confident image attracts success.

At a Pante seminar, I arrived with my three most dazzling outfits, as we were instructed. I sat and watched with awe and amazement as he transformed woman after woman into a dynamic, put-together professional. Then it was my turn. I stepped to the front of the room dressed for evaluation. Pante turned to me and said, "This looks like a housewife from Boise, Idaho." Totally devastated, I was too embarrassed to tell him it wasn't Boise, Idaho, it was Ottumwa, Iowa. Needless to say, I made major changes in my wardrobe. This experience gave me a new understanding of how your wardrobe can send messages of abundance and success.

People judge you by your clothes and your external appearance. It might not be fair, but you might as well take care of the things you can control to make a good first impression. In the first ninety seconds, people make decisions about all aspects of your life, just by judging your appearance, including clothing, hair, make-up, accessories and posture. People make decisions about your economic situation, social status, education, level of job position, type of career field and personality traits.

There are many stereotypes and behaviors that weaken a woman's professional image. In interviewing both men and women, some of the most frequently mentioned stereotypes that affect a woman's image are as follows:

Crying when angry or stressed – Crying was the most frequently mentioned image-killer. Men have been given outlets such as pounding their fists on the table, shouting loudly and even using profanity to vent their stress. Women, on the other hand, have been programmed that those behaviors are inappropriate and unfeminine. They have, however, been given permission to cry as an outlet for their stress. For specific types of stress, such as a loss of a loved one, a critical injury or the illness of a friend or family member, women have not only been given permission to cry but have been required by society to openly grieve; whereas men have been taught that big boys don't cry.

Now, I'm not advocating that we start pounding our fists on the table or take up swearing to get our frustrations out. What I am advocating is an appropriate method for maintaining your emotional control in the business environment. Using the Posture of Excellence, or other comfort management techniques, you can learn to control emotional outbursts. Admittedly, there are times when you are so angry that the only action that seems available to you is a good cry. If that's the case, find a place out of your professional environment. You can cry in the ladies' room, in the elevator or behind closed doors. Some people like to shout out their frustrations in their car or turn up the volume on the radio and sing out loud. Others will find a physical release, such as going for a walk, to remove themselves from the environment causing the frustration. My friend, Dorothy, says she growls. Yes, growls. I guess it's better than swearing.

Fidgeting with jewelry and hair – Twisting earrings, necklaces, bracelets or rings gives the appearance of nervousness or boredom. Sometimes we're not even aware that we are doing this. Continually brushing the hair out of your eyes or away from your face during a briefing or speech can distract the listener from your presentation. Choose a hairstyle that keeps your hair in place. Ask someone who has observed you if you are displaying any of these behaviors that could hurt your image.

Inappropriate dress – To dress appropriately you must first recognize what is acceptable and not acceptable in your particular work environment, the nature of the business and the visibility of your position. Look to the women who hold positions similar to your own for your lead. Another good idea is to know how women dress who are in the position you want to move into. Start dressing as though you have already been promoted. Someone who dresses as though they were going to a cocktail party instead of work is not taken seriously in the business world. Wearing low-cut dresses, dresses made of synthetic clinging material, see-through or lacy blouses, skirts with exaggerated slits, open-toed shoes with cocktail or ankle straps or metallic shoes were mentioned most often as inappropriate for the office.

If you are not sure about the professional image that you are projecting, seek professional advice. Just as you would seek advice about real estate or the stock market, seek advice on how to invest in your professional image. Find someone with whom you feel comfortable, someone who will take time to understand your current job as well as your career aspirations. Give them as much information as possible about your personal life and lifestyle. This will help them (and you) select the most appropriate clothes for work and play, clothes that your budget can support.

Wearing poor quality clothing – It is better to have three quality outfits than to have ten fair ones. Select classic styles that you can wear more than one season. Buy at the end of the season when you can find significantly marked down prices. Select fabrics that resist wrinkles and hold a fresh look. Whether it's a skirt and blouse or jeans and a tee shirt, make sure they are pressed. Avoid any slogans that may have questionable language or messages. When in doubt, save those items for when you go out on your own time. While they may be funny to your friends, they can be an image-killer in the workplace.

Balancing career and home – Inability to meet the demanding time schedule of work or travel because of family responsibilities weakens your image as a professional woman. This includes child-related responsibilities, i.e. doctor appointments, school functions and religious and community activities. It might also include caring for an elderly adult family member or household management tasks, such as waiting for a repairperson. Have a plan of action and back up support for handling family responsibilities and unexpected household demands.

Not standing when someone enters a room – Men have traditionally stood when another person enters the room, especially if that person is in a senior position, while women have traditionally remained seated. If you stay seated, this gives the appearance that you are really not there to interact but just to observe. Stand when everyone else stands.

Not shaking hands when introduced – The handshake's purpose has evolved over time from showing surrender to showing agreement and friendship. Originally, the act of shaking hands was a signal of surrender. In order to shake hands, men would have to lay down their swords. In the United States, this demonstration of cooperation extended into peacetime and the business world. When verbal agreements were made, they were finalized with a handshake. The firmer the handshake, the firmer the commitment to the agreement. It has not always been acceptable for a woman to shake hands. This act was perceived as unfeminine and reserved for men. Women were not involved in business or, if they were, a man acted upon their behalf in negotiations and finalized the agreement with a handshake. Women have extended their hand, not to show that they had put aside their sword, but for a kiss from the knight in shining armor.

Today, a handshake is a way of setting a tone of cooperation during introductions or greetings. When women shake hands, it demonstrates that they are a part of the interaction. When you extend your hand, you are also extending your personality and delivering a message to the other person. If your handshake is strong and confident, you will give the appearance of being strong and confident. Please note the difference between firm and bone breaking. You are attempting to show commitment, not inflict pain. Beware if you get a handshake from someone that brings tears to your eyes. They may be into one-upmanship on several levels. A weak or limp handshake sends a message indicating a lack of confidence, a lack of knowledge or an unwillingness to be a part of the interaction. Practice a firm handshake so you can send a message that you are a serious, confident participant.

Lack of mobility – Many women do not accept geographic moves as readily as men. In working couples, the male wage earner often determines where the family lives, as it is assumed he will have more opportunities for promotion and a higher earning potential. If you observe that senior level positions require geographic moves and you have your sights on one of those positions, let decision makers know that you are willing to meet that demand.

Playing "Girl Friday" – Cindi, who held a senior-level position in one of the largest banks in her state, was asked to serve on a statewide policy board. She discovered she was the only woman on the board. At the bi-monthly meetings, she found she was having a difficult time being recognized as a peer by the other board members. When it was time to check on the coffee or order lunch, all eyes turned to her. It was assumed, automatically, she would be the person to take care of such matters. She said she would not have minded taking care of those details, except that she felt her professional image was compromised. If she left the meeting, she would be perceived as either not being interested enough in the proceedings to stay or would contribute to the perception she was not a valuable member of the group.

One day, Cindi finally announced her commitment was to the proceedings at hand and she did not want to leave the room. After she had spoken, there was complete silence. Her colleagues mirrored looks of disbelief. Finally, one colleague spoke up. "I had just assumed, as a woman, you would know how to do those things better. I apologize."

Talking about your husband, significant other and children – If a man talks about his family or makes it known that work decisions were based on the needs of his family, he is seen as a responsible family man. He is commended for his attentiveness to family needs. A woman, on the other hand, is seen as not taking her career seriously. Putting the needs of the family first suggests that a woman will not be loyal to the organization. When a woman talks about her husband, her husband's job and their children, it is perceived that she is unable to leave the kids and husband at home and focus on her job. Learn when and how much to share about your family and home life.

Unable to articulate job capabilities – Being able to confidently articulate your job description or the contributions that your work makes to overall company goals is an image enhancer. I had a young woman, Amy, recently say to me "Oh, I'm just a secretary." I responded with, "JUST a secretary?" She blushed and said, "Well, you know what I mean." The fact is, I did not know what she meant. I didn't know where she worked or for whom. I didn't know if she was a generalist or if she specialized in a specific type of secretarial work.

If you have difficulty telling others what you do, people assume you either do it poorly or that your work must not be too important. Practice saying aloud your name, your job title and a brief overview of what you do. Just as with the handshake, project confidently who you are and what you do.

What is the one opinion you have been holding on to or the one belief you have been living by that has kept you from developing a more successful and professional image? If you gave up this opinion or belief, what new possibilities would be available to you?

In summarizing Principal and Interest, remember you first must be completely convinced you are deserving of wealth and abundance. To do this, you must eliminate any old repetitious thought patterns that have kept abundance from you. You must become aware of the profound effects of self-talk. Your thoughts determine your professional self-image and the way you manage yourself and your money.

It is all too easy to repeat money woes to ourselves and others, grinding the negativity deeper into our psyche. We want to develop and maintain a concept of ourselves as deserving of good things, and that includes wealth and status. Employing the Posture of Excellence technique will enable you to replace any negative or limiting self-talk with self-talk of abundance and prosperity.

Practice Application

Read the instructions completely so that you understand the practice application process. After you have done that, try it out!

- Get into a comfortable position with music playing softly in the background.
- Close your eyes.
- Take several deep breaths as you relax with the music.
- Search out and examine any old fears, beliefs and conditioning that keep you from becoming more attractive, more successful and financially abundant.
- Ask yourself if you gave up these opinions or beliefs, what new possibilities might be available to you.
- Let go of any fears, beliefs and conditioning that have kept you from pursuing your financial goals.
- See, hear and feel events that create abundance in your life.
- Repeat these or similar affirmations several times a week.
  - ❖ *I am deserving of the abundance of the world and all the good in it.*
  - ❖ *I am confident and capable.*
  - ❖ *I am worthy of privacy and comfort.*
  - ❖ *I am worthy of ease and luxury.*
  - ❖ *I am worthy of warmth and safety.*
  - ❖ *I am financially secure.*

> ❖ *I am able to help my friends and loved ones.*
>
> ❖ *A Promotable Woman is deserving of wealth and status.*
>
> ❖ *I am deserving of wealth and status.*
>
> ❖ *I am a Promotable Woman.*

• As you continue to relax with the music, enjoy the abundance state you have created. When you are finished, slowly stretch your arms and legs and open your eyes.

Reinforcement Activities

1. Do you have a financial plan? _____

2. How are you maintaining a long-term horizon, not just living for today?_____

   _____

3. How have you allocated your assets to include the right mix of stocks, bonds and cash? _____

   _____

4. How is your money being affected by taxes and inflation?_____

   _____

   _____

5. How can you start today to save more or invest better?_____

   _____

   _____

6. If you obtained greater wealth, what new challenges might you be faced with? _____

_____

7. How are you currently investing your financial resources in yourself, your goals and your aspirations? From what other sources can you derive income other than your job? _____

_____

_____

_____

_____

8. What does a prosperous woman look like? How does she walk, dress and talk? What are you envisioning? Can you put your face on that image? Write a description of yourself as a prosperous woman.

_____

_____

_____

_____

9. What can you do to improve your professional image? _____

_____

_____

_____

Chapter 7
Purposing

SELF-ASSESSMENT

Before reading this chapter, rate yourself on the questions listed below.

Have you created a vision of where you want to be in life?

Absolutely_____Not yet

How would you rate your ability to define and set goals?

Haven't done it _____Great

How relentless are you in the pursuit of your goals?

Not at all _____Very Relentless

How would you rate your past ability to achieve goals?

Nonexistent_____Great

How much control do you feel you have over the direction of your life?

None _____Total Control

Purposing

If you don't know where you're going, any road will get you there.
From *Alice in Wonderland*

This chapter Purposing, is my favorite topic. Purposing is goal setting, a skill you'll develop or refine in this chapter. In assessing top-level executives, surveys have identified goal setting as essential to their success. A top management consultant, Peter Vale, coined the term, "Purposing." He defines it as both purpose and action.

Castles in the Sky

Henry David Thoreau wrote,
If one advances confidently in the direction of his dreams, and endeavors to live the life which he has imagined, he will meet with a success unexpected in common hours. If you have built castles in the air, your work need not be lost; that is where they should be. Now put the foundations under them.

By employing the action steps for empowering goals, you will have laid the foundation.

And from *The Prophet* by Kahill Gibran:
Your reason and your passion are the rudder and the sails of your seafaring soul.

If either your sails or your rudder be broken, you can but toss and drift, or else be held at a standstill in mid-seas.

For reason, ruling alone, is a force confining; and passion, unattended, is a flame that burns to its own destruction.

Therefore, let your soul exalt your reason to the height of passion, that it may sing;

And let it direct your passion with reason, that your passion may live through its own daily resurrection, and like the phoenix rise above its own ashes.

Goal setting is not a new idea. There have been numerous "systems," "steps" or "processes" experts have offered that will ensure you get what you want out of life. Then why is it that goal setting is still talked about as if it were a new idea? I am sure you have set goals and achieved them. I bet you have set some goals and still are waiting for the results you had in mind. You may have had good intentions but got distracted by the demands of everyday life that kept you from the thoughts and actions that would have led you to where you wanted to be.

I quit making New Year's resolutions a long time ago. I found I would make resolutions, and even write them down. A few months later I would realize I had made these resolutions because that is what you are supposed to do after the champagne is gone and the party hats are in the garbage. I would then get depressed because I had done nothing or had just made a few feeble attempts to fulfill my resolutions.

Can you identify with this? Of course the champagne and party hats could have been a catalyst for you to let your hair down and boldly announce those dreams you had secretly held. What happened when you didn't follow through? Probably, like most of us, you beat yourself up for not holding true to your resolutions. If you did make a New Year's resolution and achieved it, you deservedly should be proud of your accomplishments. You had the resolve to follow through and might have used some or all of the steps for effective Purposing. Instead of that once a year stab at setting your life's path, think of goal setting as a skill you will build and then use every day. When you are actively involved in goal setting, you are giving your full attention and focus to your life. Be patient with yourself as you move confidently toward your goals. I have always laughed when I have heard the imposing question, "How do you eat an elephant?" The answer, of course is, "One bite at a time." Another favorite saying is, "Inch by inch it is a cinch. Yard by yard it is hard."

Long term =
   10 or more years

Medium term =
       5 to 10 years

Short term =
       1 to 5 years

Immediate action =
   daily weekly or
   monthly action

Gap Planning

Long-term goals offer the opportunity to look to the future to see where you want to be in ten to twenty years. Then think about where you are now. The "gap" between where you are and where you want to be are the action steps that you will turn into short- and medium-term goals. You can then decide what immediate actions you must take daily, weekly and monthly to move you toward your long-term goals. One approach to identifying your gaps is to complete a SWOT Analysis.

SWOT Analysis

A technique I often use with my client organizations is designed to increase their awareness of opportunities for change and innovation. It's called a SWOT (pronounced swat) Analysis. The "S" stands for strengths, the "W" for weaknesses, the "O" for opportunities, and the "T" for threats. As I began coaching individuals, I found myself asking them to identify the same components as they developed their personal leadership and performance improvement plans.

Gee, it wasn't a huge leap to recognize I could be doing that with my own goals. When I used the SWOT analysis on my own life, it revealed to me those areas I knew but kept on a more subconscious level. I hadn't accepted or acknowledged them. If I brought them to the conscious level, I might have to do something about them!

Let's start with your strengths. A strength can be thought of as a resource, particular skill, or a unique competency. Once you recognize your true strengths, you can capitalize on those strengths. A weakness refers to any aspect that may keep you from achieving a specific action step or goal. When you recognize your weaknesses, you can begin developing strategies for overcoming those weaknesses or minimizing the impact the weaknesses could have on your success. An opportunity is an infinite number of possibilities awaiting you. Identifying an opportunity is simply the process of seeing the abundance that is available to you in all aspects of your life. It is practicing Prosperity

Thinking. A threat is anything that could hinder or stop you from achieving your goals and may include a lack or void in resources or your constantly changing personal and professional environment. Take a minute to complete your personal SWOT Analysis:

My strengths are:

_____

_____

_____

My weaknesses are:

_____

_____

_____

My opportunities are:

_____

_____

_____

My threats are:

_____

_____

_____

Who Are You, Really?

Now that you have completed your SWOT Analysis, there are some other questions you need to ask yourself before you begin setting realistic goals, goals that are compatible with who you really are and what you really want out of life.

1. What do you tell yourself on a regular basis that you know is true about who you are? _____

   _____

   _____

2. What do you hold onto knowing it is really not who you are? _____

   _____

   _____

   _____

3. What image or message do you send to others that is the real you? _____

   _____

   _____

4. What image or message do you send to others that is not the real you and why do you think you send it if it is not really you? _____

   _____

Lights, Camera, Action!

It's time to explore the four action steps for empowering goals and employing Purposing:

> Action Step One: Create a vision (dream big)
> Action Step Two: Focus on what you want
> Action Step Three: Write down your goals
> Action Step Four: Repeat mental rehearsals

Create a Vision (Dream the Impossible Dream)

Let's begin with Action Step One: Create a vision. Creating a Vision is your ability to formulate creative ideas on a large scale. It is really the ability to dream the impossible and then turn it into the possible. This may seem scary at first, but if you aim high, even if you fall short, you have already accomplished a great deal. Feel free to shoot for the stars and believe your dreams will come true.

Dreaming comes easier to some of us than to others. Children do it easily. Were you ever caught daydreaming? Most of us were and as children we were programmed that daydreaming was a negative activity and we never wanted to be caught doing it.

Don't Get Caught by the Daydreaming Police

Yet, as children, we were able to easily remove ourselves from the here and now and project ourselves into another time and place in our imagination. As adults, most of us have lost our ability to daydream. Daydreaming is more than an idle escape from the moment; it's really a way of opening your mind to the many options available on your life's journey. And because daydreaming is very private, it allows us to explore options that we might not openly share with others. There's no one saying, "Are you kidding, at your age?" or "With your training?" or "Where are you going to get the money?" or "But you've never done anything like that before!" or "But they only hire from the inside," and so on and so on. As soon as you put your dream out in front of someone else, you have to be prepared to hear other people's fears and their limiting self-talk squelching your vision.

Guess the Daydreaming Police Got Them

At one of my first The Promotable Woman: What Makes The Difference training programs, two women came up to me and said that the program was not for professional women if words like daydreaming were to be used. They said daydreaming was more suited to teenagers thinking about a person of the opposite sex or anticipating the school dance. Even though I had also used words like "mission" and "goals" and "vision," I wondered why they had only heard "daydreaming," clearly a case of selective hearing and focusing on their negative view of daydreaming. Were they victims of the daydreaming police and had they paid the price for being caught?

Had they lost their ability to daydream or failed to realize the importance that such activity plays in shaping our lives? Had they dreamed and not reached their dream or had they experienced negative feedback from others when they shared their dream? It did serve to remind me how strong our cultural biases are and how many of our natural creative processes have been suppressed by the reactions we receive from others.

It is true that you cannot spend all of your time daydreaming, escaping from reality or avoiding decisions about your career or commitments to relationships. But, properly employed, daydreaming can be a useful tool. Daydreaming is the first step in establishing your mission, your path, your life's purpose. It gives you permission to explore all possibilities without judgment, criticism or limitations. It is an opportunity to focus on an abundance of positive expectations.

From Cooking and Carpools to Careers

I recall one of the first classes I taught at a community college. This particular class was made up mostly of women who were going back into the workplace after several years at home raising the children or managing the household. Some were suffering the empty-nest syndrome and wanted to go back to work. Others had suddenly found themselves divorced or widowed after fifteen, twenty or twenty-five years of marriage. Their motivations may have been different, but their goals were the same: They wanted to be productive members of the workforce. However, they lacked self-confidence or a personal identity and they had lost their ability to see into the future – their ability to daydream. They had been so busy taking care of the here and now, they became stuck somewhere between the past and the future. Their future had been programmed as they committed their energies to supporting their husbands' careers and raising their children.

My challenge was to provide an environment where these women could rediscover their ability to daydream, to explore options, and to analyze ways of creating positive change in their lives. They had to become comfortable in moving outside their comfort zone so they could set realistic and meaningful personal and career goals.

Standing Ovation, Please

As I was challenging these women to daydream, and then to take the necessary action to turn those daydreams into a reality, I remembered my own daydreams about an unknown future. I was filled with excitement and anticipation as I explored these future possibilities. Years ago, when I was a teller at a large utility and hadn't yet received my teaching degree, my most frequent daydream involved seeing myself in front of large, adult audiences, giving speeches and, of course, feeling the excitement of the applause of the crowd. Later, as a junior high school teacher, I would justify that I was indeed making presentations to large audiences, my students. There was no applause and there was no standing ovation, just students standing to get out of the classroom as fast as possible. Yet, deep down I knew this wasn't really my vision and that I would eventually leave my junior high students for adult audiences.

The Going Away School

Just as daydreaming took me from the teller window to the speaking platform, curiosity and daydreaming took a Navajo boy from an isolated area of a reservation in Arizona to become a world-renowned figure in nuclear physics. When Fred Begay was nine years old, living in Monument Valley, Arizona, he asked his mother what made a rainbow. He told me he was always curious about natural phenomena and was continually bombarding his mother with questions that she couldn't answer. When he persisted with his questions about the rainbow, she said, "You'll have to ask the teacher at the Going Away School." The Going Away School was a three-day walk across the desert wilderness. With his pack and a three-day supply of food, nine-year-old Fred Begay anxiously set out alone on his journey of discovery.

When he arrived at the Going Away School, the teacher was explaining the rules and regulations of the school and paused to ask if there were any questions. This was his opportunity, so he raised his hand and asked his question, assuming that once he had his answer, he would return home. So he posed his question about the rainbow to the teacher. The teacher dismissed his curiosity with, "You'll learn that in science class later." I asked Fred when he finally found out what made the rainbow work. He said, fifteen years later, while working on his physics degree.

Fred's mother not only gave him permission to dream, but encouraged him to pursue answers to his questions.

This pursuit took him from the Navajo reservation to a leadership position at Los Alamos National Laboratories.

In this chapter, you not only have permission to dream, but dreaming will be required as you begin setting your goals. What are your most cherished lifetime dreams, personally, spiritually, financially, professionally?

Make these lifetime or long-term goals BIG so that more immediate or short-term goals will fit into them. If you make goals too narrow, it's difficult to expand them. Think like Ma Joad, in Steinbeck's depression-era book *The Grapes of Wrath*. In packing up all her worldly goods to fit on the top of the old car that was to take the family from the dust bowl of Oklahoma to California, she decided to take only large pots and pans, leaving all the little ones behind. She reasoned, "You can always put a little bit in a big pot, but you can't put a lot in a little pot." When you are dreaming big, you can do only what you can imagine, so let your imagination run wild. Have a broad, sweeping vision of what you want.

Focus On What You Want (Raise Your Head and See the Coastline)

This brings us to the Second Action Step: Focus on what you want. Have a clear vision of your goal to pull you toward where you're going. One of the best examples of goal setting is the story of Florence Chadwick, who attempted to swim the Catalina Channel. On a foggy and overcast day, she set out and swam and swam. After fifteen hours and fifty-five minutes, she gave up less than one-half mile from land. She said if she could have seen the coastline, she could have made it. With her goal still in focus, she decided to try again, but this time she started out on a clear day. She swam and swam and every time she was tired and wanted to stop, she would raise her head out of the water to see the coastline. Just seeing the coastline would give her a new surge of energy. She successfully swam the channel!

Just as Florence Chadwick had a clear vision of the coastline to pull her toward her goal, you should focus clearly on what you want in all aspects of your life. Set your own coastline.

When I asked what you wanted financially, did you ask yourself, "Does she mean this summer's vacation, the children's college tuition or my retirement needs?" These questions point out that different goals have different motivations and deadlines. By deadline I mean that goals can be long-term, medium-term, short-term or immediate action goals.

An interesting side note is, in working with both men and women on goal setting, there was a difference in how they related their goals to me. Some could easily relate their goals, while others said they either didn't have goals or their goals were not clearly defined. When men shared their goals, their vision of their future in their personal life and careers, they talked about what they were doing to make it happen. Almost without exception, they would talk about what they wanted. Women, almost without exception, talked about what they didn't want.

When thinking about their future, men saw abundance

and practiced Prosperity Thinking. They focused on what they were moving toward instead of what they were moving away from. Going back to Prosperity Thinking, a critical skill for you is to be able to focus on what you want to go toward, not away from what you don't want.

Write Down Your Goals

Having your goals clearly in mind is establishing your purpose. Remember purposing means purpose and action. The act of writing down your goals, which is Action Step Three, adds even more power to them. You make a contract with yourself when you write down your goals. Think seriously about some goals in specific areas. As you think about these goals, visualize yourself successfully achieving the goals.

Mom, I Have Them Right Here

One day my son, Josh, was sharing with me ideas he had for starting his own business. He enthusiastically talked about what he would have to do until he could swing leaving his employer and going out on his own. He had thought through many of the specifics, including how many employees he would need to start, what training he would need to pass licensing tests, how long it might take before he had the money for equipment and tools, and much more. I asked him if he had written his goals. When he said he hadn't, I offered to help him write out a few goals so he could look at them everyday as a motivator. He said (as he tapped the side of his head), "I don't have to write them down. I have them right here." Later that same day when his uncle asked me how Josh was doing, I told him of Josh's plans for his business. He asked if Josh had written out his goals and when I said he hadn't, he said, "Tell Josh as long as they are in his mind they are a dream, but when he writes them down, they are a business plan." Simple words, but a great way to summarize the importance of taking goals from the nebulous to success.

Your goals (and your self-talk) must be worded correctly. The rules for writing goals are explicit. When you incorporate the following four components, you are personalizing and adding specifics to the outcome. Goals should be written:

- First person, singular (I)
- Present tense (Write your goals "I am" rather than past tense, "I have" or future tense, "I will")
- As if they have already happened (Not that you want something, but that what you want, you already have)
- Using words that are full of energy and create a sense of happiness, contentment, pride, accomplishment and fun!

By writing your goals in first person, you have not only made a contract with yourself, but you have also accepted the responsibility for the goal. If you set a goal worded "we" or "he" or "she," there is a natural tendency to place the responsibility for achieving the goal on the other person.

There is also a tendency to blame other people or external circumstances when a goal is not achieved. Writing goals in second or third person may make you feel as if you're not in control of your own destiny. When you say "I," it puts you in control of the outcome of your life.

Writing your goals in present tense makes goal setting an active process. If you write them in past tense such as "I have lost ten pounds," your conscious and subconscious say, "Good! Now I don't have to do anything else." Or, better yet, "Bring on the chocolates!" When your goal is worded in future tense, such as "I will start my diet tomorrow," tomorrow never comes. Whenever I hear people wording their goals in future tense, I always think of a sign in a local pub that says, "Free beer tomorrow."

When you write your goals as if you were enjoying the success of their accomplishment, it adds excitement and vitality to your purpose. That is why you want to include positive, emotionally charged words in your affirmations to help you "feel" the results you want. Include visually descriptive words so you can "see" your results, and include words that let you "hear" about your success. Also, it is a good idea to add action words, making your goal come alive in your imagination. Use language that is vivid and detailed. Put a due date on your goals to help pull you toward your "coastline." I recommend you don't put a due date on personality, spiritual or relationship goals. These goals should be ongoing, changing and evolving with your own growth rather than having a finite end.

INEFFECTIVE GOAL: I want to lose fifteen pounds.

EMPOWERING GOAL: I am a slim, trim and healthy _____ pounds.

Remember the old saying, "Be careful what you ask for, because you'll probably get it," I added "healthy" to my weight loss goal. I don't want to lose fifteen pounds through illness.

INEFFECTIVE GOAL: I will save 15 percent of my income this year.

EMPOWERING GOAL: I am enjoying reading my savings account balance of $_____ on December 3lst. (Your short-term or monthly goal will be: I am enjoying the monthly increase of $_____ in my savings account balance.)

INEFFECTIVE GOAL: I will be Vice President of Marketing in two years.

EMPOWERING GOAL: On June 10 I am filled with pride and a sense of accomplishment as I send out letters to friends and colleagues announcing my promotion to Vice President of Marketing.

INEFFECTIVE GOAL: I want to get my real estate license.

EMPOWERING GOAL: On October 24 I am hanging my newly received real estate license on my office wall.

INEFFECTIVE GOAL: We are buying a house in three years.

EMPOWERING GOAL: I am enjoying having

breakfast in the sun-filled country kitchen of my new 4-bedroom, passive-solar home in the mountains on May 5.

INEFFECTIVE GOAL: I want to quit smoking.

People typically write: "I am a nonsmoker" or "I'm not smoking cigarettes any more." Although written correctly in present tense, goals should move you toward your desired outcome instead of away from what you don't want. Each time you use the word "smoking" or "cigarettes," it brings a visual image of you as a smoker.

EMPOWERING GOAL: I am only breathing in clean, fresh air. I am developing habits that create good health.

INEFFECTIVE GOAL: We're going on vacation to Germany next year.

EMPOWERING GOAL: I am enjoying traveling in the beautiful German countryside in September. I am enjoying traveling with my family as we explore historical landmarks of Germany.

Speaking of Germany, get a passport. Not only is it now required if you are going to be traveling across most country borders (including Canada and Mexico), you are prepared for any opportunities for vacations or work assignments that might involve international travel. Ready for new adventures and ready to expand your knowledge and experiences, it may be the best money you spend, even though there are no immediate plans that require a passport. Ready for life's turn of events, you are in control. Having a passport is a way of anticipating positive outcomes. It's Prosperity Thinking!

You should also pay attention to how a goal feels. Does it feel right? A hunch is your intuition trying to tell you something.

You've dreamed big, you've focused specifically on what you want, you've learned the steps for writing goals, and now you'll add more power to them by actually writing them. I suggest you begin by simply using 3 x 5 notecards to familiarize yourself with the process. On one side of a card, write one long-term goal. On the other, write step-by-step actions you will need to do to achieve the long-term goal. These will be your short- and medium-term goals, along with any daily, weekly or monthly steps necessary.

The first time I heard of this process was during a seminar I attended. I thought, "Give me a break! I'm not in elementary school." But I reluctantly went along with the activity. To my surprise, it was harder than I thought to take a long-term goal from a flood of images into more manageable steps to get to my end result. Having only the space of a 3 x 5 card, I had to really focus on which actions to take and what order of priority would be the most effective. The more I worked to reduce my long-term goal to one notecard, the more clearly I could define and write succinct action steps.

Once you have your notecards, you can create a file on your computer, your PDA or any other tool so you can review your goals anytime, anywhere. You may want to create a flowchart giving you a quick glance at the steps you will need to take.

Don't throw away those notecards. In fact, make duplicate sets and keep one set in your desk, one in your briefcase, one in your car and one at home. Have them within reach so any spare moments can be used to reinforce your priority action steps. When stopped in traffic, on hold on the phone, riding the subway, waiting for appointments or airplanes, or simply suffering from a case of the irrelevancies, review your goal cards and give yourself a boost. You may want to find a picture, or several pictures, that represent the end result of your action steps or the "you of the future" and use them as screensavers.

A technique I've used is to paste my goal cards on the wall over my desk along with pictures from magazines that represent my wish with a due date. A few years ago I had a picture of a sailboat over my desk. I wanted to hold my next annual corporate meeting on a sailboat. Kathy, my new Vice President of Operations at the time, asked me about the affirmation picture on my wall. After a brief explanation, the subject was dropped. Three weeks later Kathy announced she had told her friend, a sailboat dealer, of my affirmation. He was so fascinated with the concept of affirmations he offered a boat and crew at no charge for our annual meeting! My new affirmation is to always include Kathy in my affirmations. While I didn't have the corporate meeting on a sailboat, I did have the opportunity to continue my work with dolphins and we happened to spend a week on the ocean in a sailboat, one that looked eerily like the one in my picture.

Another technique coming back into practice is creating a collage of multiple goals. Simply get a piece of posterboard and fill it with pictures of your goal's end result. Create one unique picture, design or set of words that represent your overall life's vision or dream.

Several years after the sailboat "incident," Kathy opened her own consulting firm and shares this story of how a collage impacted her career.

Kathy's Fast Forward

I am a strong believer in the theory that success is 80 percent mental preparation and 20 percent action! About eleven years ago I started a new business and before I officially launched my business I put together a "vision board." I thought carefully about where I wanted to be personally and professionally. Because I'm a visual person, I sat down with a stack of magazines and a large posterboard and created my vision of my ideal future. I also wrote affirmations on my board and on a daily basis affirmed my goals.

My "vision board" kept me grounded and optimistic as I managed the daily challenges and opportunities of running a small business. One thing was incredibly consistent – my business thrived. Even when other small businesses were struggling with economic pressures my business flourished. The right people appeared at the right time, new ideas and opportunities came easily to me, I didn't have to do "cold calling" because people called me!

Then an interesting thing happened as I was moving my business to a larger space and unpacking my boxes – my "vision board" reappeared!

I gingerly opened it up, as it had been packed away for over seven years, and laid it out on my desk. As my eyes glanced over each photo and handwritten affirmation, I realized all of my goals had been accomplished and, in many cases, exceeded! It was like the universe continued to work on my goals even when they weren't in front of me.

Think Outside the Box and Then Put It In a Box

Yet another technique is to get a box such as a shoe box, file box or any other container where you can put items that represent your goals. If you want a new car, go to the hardware store and buy a blank key with the car's brand name on it. If you are working on a fitness plan get a membership card from a local fitness center, a shoestring from a running shoe, a clothing tag with that "new size" or a picture of yourself when you were in ideal physical condition and put them in the box. If you are working on a financial goal, include fake money, pictures of what you will have when you have reached your financial goal. Perhaps it is a copy of a diploma or certificate that you hope for, which could also relate to a career or educational goal. Do you see how they may all be interrelated? Occasionally look into the box and see how you're progressing.

Talking to Yourself? We All Knew You Were a Little Strange!

You've thought about your goals, you've learned a technique for writing them and now you're going to add even more power to them by incorporating Action Step Four: Repeat mental rehearsals into the goal setting process. Repeated mental rehearsals allow you to see yourself during each step on the way to achieving your goals and to see yourself enjoying the final outcome. Repeating goals aloud are called affirmations, which is simply the process of affirming to be true the mental images you have created about the future you. Affirmations re-energize your efforts. They demonstrate your ability to take thoughts and put them into words.

Make a special electronic file, folder or scrapbook where you can permanently retire your goal cards, photos or collages after each goal is completed. Have a document on your computer or PDA that you can call up that includes photos or images of your goal accomplishments. Whenever doubts about success start sabotaging your Prosperity Thinking and Purposing activities, simply open your file or look in your folder or scrapbook to remind yourself that you have successfully set and achieved goals in the past and you certainly will be successful again as you continue working on your goals.

The ability to set and achieve goals is essential to your happiness and success. Striving to achieve goals puts you in charge of your life. Goal setting is an active process for change that leads to tangible results. It is a tool that guides you from daydreaming to reality and the rewards of your efforts. Every time you achieve even one action step on the way to your long-range goal, it makes you stronger. Seeing your progress is a great motivator to make more changes, take more risks and dig into more of your action steps.

Take A Bow

Reward yourself positively when you accomplish even the smallest step toward your goal. Rewards can be as simple as putting a big red circle around your goal. Other people want tangible rewards such as treating themselves to a weekend in the mountains, a massage or taking the day off to visit their favorite museum. The type of reward isn't as important as the process of acknowledging your successes.

Come to the Edge and You Surely Will Fly

We can make all the wishes we want, have our "coastline" clearly in mind, set due dates, and even write down your goals, but we must have the follow-through to make those wishes become a reality. This is the time for persistence. It calls for the relentless pursuit of your dreams. Pursuing your dreams may involve taking risks. Think about the times that you took a risk. It has been said that the only way we make progress is by taking the risk to step out of our comfort zone. What is the worst thing that could happen if you took a risk? What is the best thing that could happen? You just might "fly."

Come to the edge.
We might fall.
Come to the edge.
It's too high!
Come to the edge!
And they came.
And he pushed ...
and they flew.

Christopher Logue

Stop the Clock

Time management and setting priorities go hand in hand with goal setting. Ask yourself several times a day, "Is what I am doing right this moment supporting my goals?" If the answer is yes, keep doing it! If the answer is no, STOP doing it and reassess how you can move back into the thoughts and actions that will support your goals. You are pro-actively driving your future outcomes.

Set aside time daily to focus on your goals. Mentally rehearse the daily, weekly and monthly action steps you have written and visualize your final outcome. Successful people have shared with me how they include in their daily schedules time to reflect on their goals and visualize positive outcomes. What is the best time of day for you to set aside time to affirm your goals? Where will you do your affirmations? When will you start? (The correct answer is today!)

For practice, select one goal that came to mind as we discussed the goal setting process. Use that goal as your "coastline." Remember Florence Chadwick and her clear vision of the coastline that pulled her to her destination? During any affirmation activity, state your affirmation in first person, present tense, and as if it has already happened. When you do this, you are affirming to yourself not what you want, but that what you want you already have. You must be completely convinced from this point forward that you are worthy of each and every goal you have set. If you have any doubts about how your goals should be written, go back and review the examples earlier in this chapter.

Instead of repeating old tapes of failure, you will create new positive self-talk tapes. You have achieved many goals in the past, which is evidence you have the creativity, discipline and resolve to do so again in the future. During the following Posture of Excellence activity you will have the opportunity to prepare for the successful achievement of your goals.

Practice Application

Read the instructions completely so that you understand the practice application process. After you have done that, try it out!

- Get into a comfortable position with music playing softly in the background.
- Close your eyes.
- Take several deep breaths as you relax with the music.
- Silently repeat your cue word or phrase as you move into your Posture of Excellence.
- Start by thinking about long-term goals (five to ten year goals). What are your long-term goals financially? In your career? In your personal relationships? Get in touch with what you want out of life.
- As though watching a mental movie, see yourself successfully completing the goal event by event, step by step. Remember, your goals should be in first person, present tense as if they have already happened. This will allow you to internalize the feeling that you already have what you want.
- See, feel, hear and touch the experience of achieving your goal.
- Pause for a moment to congratulate yourself on each small success.
- As the music continues, visualize and refine your goal until you successfully reach it. Having achieved

Your affirmation should be stated not as what you want, but that what you want you already have.

173

the goal in your mind, take a few minutes to watch and listen to yourself enjoying your success. Feel the emotions, the pleasure, the fulfillment.

• Hear yourself sharing your accomplishment with a friend. Repeat to yourself these or similar affirmations:

> ❖ *I am pleased with many past successes.*
> ❖ *I am focusing on attitudes of success.*
> ❖ *I am confidently using my professional skills.*
> ❖ *I am capable and deserving of achieving my goals.*
> ❖ *A Promotable Woman sets and achieves her goals.*
> ❖ ***I am a Promotable Woman***

• Remain relaxed with you eyes closed as you continue to feel good about your successes. Then, whenever you are ready, slowly stretch your arms and legs, feeling energized and wide awake with renewed vitality. Your zest and enthusiasm will carry you forward as you reach you fullest potential in achieving your goals as a **Promotable Woman**.

Reinforcement Activities

Your Coastlines

1. Mark each coastline as to importance in your life right now. This will enable you to focus more clearly on the areas where you should be setting goals.

Coastline	Of Some Importance	Important	Very Important	Essential
Appearance/Image				
Personality/Habits				
Housing				
Family/Relationships				
Leisure Time				
Play/Physical				
Education				

2. In reviewing Purposing, what are the four Action Steps for empowering goals?

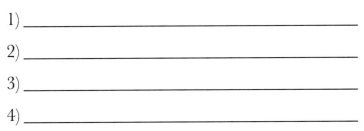

1) _____

2) _____

3) _____

4) _____

3. The four-part system for writing goals are that they must be stated:

1) _____

2) _____

3) _____

4) _____

4. What are some of your long-term dreams or visions of your success?

Personally: _____

_____

_____

Professionally: _____

_____

_____

5. Referring back to your coastlines, circle the areas you marked as essential. These are goals that have a top priority in your life.

6. Write these top priority goals as if they have already happened. Make sure the first two words of your written goal are, "I am."

I am_____

_____

I am_____

_____

I am_____

_____

7. What goals would you like to achieve within one year?

_____

_____

_____

_____

8. Describe your ideal screensaver.

_____

_____

_____

_____

_____

_____

Congratulations, You Did It!!!

You have just finished exploring the factors that have made the difference in the lives of successful people and the issues that are specific to women's successes. My hope is that you have learned more about yourself, your personal needs and your professional goals as you have read this book and completed the activities for each chapter.

May you climb the ladder of success with your binoculars focused on an incredible, prosperous and happy future so that you can look over your shoulder and exclaim, "I *HAVE* come a long way, baby!"

About the Author

Dr. Jan Northup, founder and president of Management Training Systems, Inc. (MTS), is an internationally known author, speaker, organizational strategist, training specialist and personal business coach. For more than 25 years Jan has assisted organizations, from small family-owned businesses to Fortune 100 companies. They have drawn on her expertise in working with top- and mid-level managers in the areas of strategic planning, transitional planning, quality improvement and talent management and performance enhancement.

As a professional behavioral and values analyst, Jan has assisted organizations in meeting employee development needs in subjects including mentoring, conflict resolution, team building, male/female relationships in the workplace and project planning. Jan created **The Promotable Woman: What Makes the Difference** video training program, which has been featured on the Public Broadcasting Service. She has been the featured speaker at numerous regional and national conferences and was the first woman to conduct a nationwide speaking tour of Australia on women's management issues. Jan has made frequent radio and television appearances and has written numerous articles discussing the factors that make a difference in the lives of successful people and organizations.

At the same time, she has kept her ties with academia by developing and teaching undergraduate and graduate courses in the areas of organizational design, team building, leadership and marketing. An on-line course developer and instructor in the College of Professional Studies for Bellevue University, Jan also has taught at Thunderbird, The Garvin School of International Management and at George Washington University. She has served on the Board of Directors for various organizations and has been the recipient of numerous awards and commendations for her professional and community accomplishments.

Dr. Northup's book, ***Life's A Bitch And Then You Change Your Attitude, 5 Secrets to Taming Life's Roller Coaster and Building Resilience*** examines personal and organizational resilience. Jan contributes to ***Speaking of Success***, a compilation of success strategies, with Ken Blanchard, Stephen Covey, Jack Canfield and other leading authorities and to ***Rising To The Top*** with Jim Rohn, Patricia Ball, Les Brown and others.

Contact Us

Please contact Dr. Northup for additional copies of ***The Promotable Woman: Have We Come A Long Way, Baby?*** or if you are looking for:

- A keynote speaker
- Corporate training
- An organizational strategist
- A business or career coach or
- Talent recruiting and management.

Management Training Systems, Inc.
P.O. Box 11806
Glendale, AZ 85318

623-587-7644

www.trainingperformance.com

www.thebizcoach4u.com